THE
NEW
MARRIAGE

*Transcending the
Happily-Ever-After Myth*

How to Put Your
Relationship Back on Track

Linda Miles, PH. D.
and
Robert Miles, M. D.

Cypress House

The New Marriage:
Transcending the Happily-Ever-After Myth
Copyright ©2000 by Robert and Linda Miles

Edited by Julie Voich and Martin Terrell

Cypress House
155 Cypress Street
Fort Bragg, CA 95437
(800) 773-7782
www.cypresshouse.com

Cover design and illustration: Michael Brechner/Cypress House
Front cover: original photographs: ©1999 by Jay Odee
Back cover: author photograph: Beverly Frick Photography

Disclaimer: The names, identifying features and circumstances
of the clients discussed in this book have been altered
to protect their confidentiality and privacy.

Library of Congress Cataloging-in Publication Data

Miles, Linda, 1947 Jan. 3-
        The new marriage : transcending the happily-ever-after myth : how
to put your relationship back on track / Linda Miles and Robert Miles.
                p. cm.
        Includes bibliographical references.
        ISBN 1-879384-39-6 (pbk.)
        1. Marriage 2. Marriage--Psychological aspects.
3. Communication in marriage. I. Miles, Robert, 1937- II. Title.
HQ734 .M5643 2000
306.81 -- dc21   00-031481

Manufactured in the USA
First edition
2   4   6   8   9   7   5   3

Dedication

To Our Children

Acknowledgments

———◇❧❦◇———

This book was a team effort. Thanks for the excellent editing by Martin Terrell, Julie Voich, and Paul Laffon. Thanks to Cypress House and John Fremont, without whose expert guidance we could not have pulled this project together. Thanks also to Dr. Joy Evans, Olivia and Bill Bilenky, Terry Benson, Liane Leshne, and Sister Christine Kelly for their feedback and encouragement. Dr. Joy Evans wrote the practical section on the use of dreams, based on her knowledge and twenty-five years of experience. Steve and Brenda Meisburg contributed the section on the Enneagram, utilizing their extensive training on this instrument.

Genie McBurnett had many creative suggestions about the use of relevant metaphors. Cassandra Harbin brought the editors and authors together and provided invaluable organizational and marketing advice. Film producer Lex Mathews spent hours doing interviews. The material about the Prodigal Son was inspired by lectures given by Dr. Francis Vanderwall and Dr. John Gottman.

Thanks also to our clients, for all that they have taught us. We are blessed by our marriage, which has taught us to live the questions.

Contents

Two are better than one;
because they have a good reward for their labor.
For if they fall,
the other one will lift up his fellow...

Ecclesiastes 4:9

Introduction

M arriage, as we have known it, is dead. Between fifty and sixty percent of today's marriages end in divorce. The divorce rate for second marriages is even higher. Many couples live in dead relationships, their unions destined for failure from the beginning. Fewer people than ever before stay together until "death do them part." What is happening to relationships? How have they gotten so far off course, and what can we do to get them back on track?

In this country, the past hundred years have brought about dramatic changes in the nature of marriage and committed relationships. At the turn of the twentieth century, life expectancy was half what it is today. It was common for young wives to die in childbirth and for families to die from the rigors of frontier life or from infectious diseases. So many women died in childbirth a few generations ago that a new religion, the Shakers, was formed in protest. In his family history, *Polk's Folly*, William R. Polk writes: "Not only was the act of giving birth a significant killer, but even unexceptional pregnancy lowered resistance, so that many normally healthy women succumbed to such common sicknesses as 'fevers and bloudie Flixe.' As a consequence, marriages seldom lasted more than a decade..." Due to life's hardships and the physical demands of making a living, a couple had little time to spend together. For most people, the mere struggle to survive made the notion of spending "quality time" together incomprehensible. Marriage was more often than not an economic contract; love had little or nothing to do with it. Women were expected to stay home with the children while the men worked the land. Most people felt old at forty.

The kinds of values we once had won't work anymore, because things are different now. As infectious diseases were conquered, people began to live longer. They became less bound together by economic necessity. Women no longer stay in groups with other women with children; they have entered the work force in nearly every area, and many are economically independent of their husbands. Men were expected to earn a living and go fight wars, not come home and have a relationship. Now men are expected to come home and listen empathetically to women. John Gottman says that the men in relationships that work well have emotionally wised up.

We can have better relationships with each other now than were possible in the past. Just look at the changes: We don't have such large families anymore, which means there are fewer children to serve as buffers. We don't have the large extended families we once had either. Couples are now turning to each other to get their needs met. In-laws and grandparents are no longer in the next room or just across the hall. Couples have learned to rely on each other in ways that earlier generations never imagined. Marriages are changing because there is a real shift in terms of what's expected in relationships.

Expectations about romantic love in marriage began to change with improvements in sanitation and living conditions. As a consequence of the Industrial Revolution, and with the unionization of labor, people migrated to cities and found jobs that provided them with disposable incomes and free time. Courtly love, once the sole province of the aristocracy, was transformed by the magic of Hollywood into romantic love, accessible to everyone. By the middle of the twentieth century, the decoding of the female reproductive cycle made family planning possible. Coupled with the outlawing of gender discrimination in employment, increased freedom in general, and the new-age emphasis on personal fulfillment, many relationships have foundered and failed.

Families became more transient due to changes in the job market, contributing to the breakup of the extended family. Couples became more isolated, with fewer children and a greater need to lean on one another. Women entered the job market in great numbers, and feminists demanded economic, social, and sexual equality regardless of gender. Accelerated change put pressure on couples to be all things to one another, a safe haven in an insecure world. New skills were called for that neither partner knew how to deliver. How does one learn to communicate, share feelings, achieve intimacy, experience compassion, identify problems, compromise, or reach consensus?

Couples actually need two contracts nowadays: one for the marriage relationship and one for co-parenting. You can break your marriage contract, but that doesn't mean you've broken your contract to co-parent. When people tell us they are leaving their children, we say, "No, you're not leaving your children; you're leaving your wife or husband." It's not that people today are any less committed to their children, it's just that women have more options now. In the past, if the man left, everybody might starve because families were almost totally reliant on the man's economic strength. Women couldn't get credit, couldn't vote, inherit wealth, or earn a living except in very prescribed situations. There are more options today. Children can be cared for and both partners can work and be financially secure. We think that humans are evolving, and that the nature of being a parent is changing.

We're looking at a new model, a new evolution, and it's going to look different from past models. Couples are going to turn to each other more for their emotional needs, which is going to require men to become more emotionally savvy than they've ever been.

Today's couple needs a relationship glossary and a map of love's territory. That's where we come in. Based on our own life experience, and that of hundreds of couples we have treated in the past twenty-five years, we wrote this book to help you make sense of your suffering and to teach you how to enjoy the benefits of a deep, meaningful relationship with your partner. This book will provide you with the tools you'll need to build, maintain and expand your relationship, if that is what you truly need. A long-term relationship is not realistic for everyone, however. Obviously, in our culture, couples are not doing a good job of staying committed. Of people who married in the 1990s, 67 percent are going to end up divorcing. Probabilities don't look so good. However, we think that people are poorly informed and haven't developed good skills for making their relationships work. We always feel bad when we go to a wedding of youngsters in their early twenties, because we realize that they're just repeating what the minister says to them. They have no idea what the whole thing really means. People grow and mature in ways that can move them far apart, and individual growth can interfere with a relationship. For example, a couple who married right out of college—before they really matured or knew themselves—might well find, ten years later, that they're totally different people, unable to bridge their differences and make the relationship work.

This doesn't necessarily mean that we should have diminished expectations of first marriages. We should recognize that marriage isn't easy, and learn about the traps and pitfalls that can destroy relationships. After all, we've written this book to let people know there's a drop-off into the valley. We want people to realize that they're going to start finding fault with each other and will probably sink into shame and blame. But we also want them to know that those things are part of a recognized cycle and can be overcome.

Second marriages aren't necessarily more successful than first marriages, but can be more successful if people have learned to face their own issues and deal with the tigers in the valley. Linda and Robert's is a second marriage, and is decidedly more successful because they did the necessary work. If people learn to deal with things without shame and blame and without faultfinding, they're definitely much better off. If, however, what they did was avoid the valley the first time around, they're no better off than they were in their first marriage.

What really worries us is when someone comes in and says, "My spouse was just a jerk, so I got a divorce." Then we know they didn't learn from their first marriage. They think that they're a cupcake who played no part in the marriage's destruction. Those people have no better chance at it the second or third time around, because each time they think they just married the wrong person.

Some people might be better off just not having a relationship, but statistically there are risk factors involved. People who are alone are more at risk for suicide and for an early death, but there are some people who do just fine outside of a relationship. The majority of us, however, need close contact with other people, however we find it.

Positive touch is so important that it can help bring your blood pressure down, which we have seen happen with older people. Renee Spitz conducted studies in orphanages where they couldn't figure out why babies died despite being fed and changed. Spitz was the first one to identify the reason those babies were dying: they needed to be held, and if they weren't held, they'd die. So there is definitely a physiological need for positive touch, which is why we stay at such risk if we stay in a bad relationship. Often,

4

you're isolated in that bad relationship and you can't get to places where you're nourished and acknowledged, and you start compromising your health.

Some relationships may simply need to end, and you must be the final judge of that. If you're living in a dead relationship, long past resuscitation, this book may bring home that realization. We designed this guide to help you create a relationship that is alive and full of joy, but you won't find any easy ways to bring a dead marriage back to life. We believe that a true marriage is a mystical union that requires much practice and preparation to survive in the modern world.

From time to time, people have asked us what we think about "open marriage." Having done this work for so long, we think we've seen just about everything, but we've never seen an open marriage save a relationship or succeed over time. It interferes with the essentials that make a relationship work: attending to your partner, letting your partner know how valuable he or she is to you, fostering their dreams and promoting what's important to them. There needs to be a real commitment to each other and to mutual growth. We think it's difficult to sustain that while also trying to maintain another relationship.

Other books focus on achieving success, winning friends, acquiring wealth, and preserving health. Here, we are concerned with relating intimately and being deeply loved. Metaphorically speaking, this is a guidebook to help you find your way through desert and jungle to the top of love's mountain. We will point out the dangers and detours, and keep you on the right path. There are many paths; the easiest leading from a loving, secure childhood. However, not everyone is lucky enough to have had good role models. What we don't learn from our parents, we learn from our peers and our experiences, and this book will help you distinguish positive from negative directions, suggest ways to right the wrongs, and turn your life around so that true love and meaningful commitment are attainable.

If your relationship is not moribund, this book will help it grow and last. If your relationship has lost its way, this book will help put it back on course. It is your guide, your map to the journey of lasting love. It is not intended to replace good counseling, but not everyone will need counseling. If used correctly, this guide will help you know where you are going and provide a road map for getting there. After all, as William Blake attests, "men and women are not alien creatures…we all want the same things."

"Marriage is a lived experience," says Sister Christine Kelly, a colleague and close friend, expressing a major theme of this book. In order to have a lived experience, you must be alive, which means you must be in touch with your feelings and your unique needs. If you are dead and do not realize it, you cannot realize that your marriage is dead. To be fully alive you must live in the present. The Greek word for "spirit" is *breath*. We must be in the present moment to fully experience a mystical union. As defined in some dictionaries, *spirit* was originally thought of as the "animating vapor infused by the breath or as bestowed by a deity." True unions are present, animated, and connect us to forces greater than ourselves. Bear in mind, however, that there may come a time when a couple should give up: when their marriage is dead and when there's no life left between them. Sister Christine also said that marriage is for life, and when there's no life left, there's no marriage left. John Gottman found that the most often-reported reason for a dying marriage was not because couples fought too often or because there'd been an affair, but because they grew apart and there was deadness between them.

Most of us are, to some extent, prisoners of the past. Our life is a small prison cell. Based on fear, ignorance, and outmoded behaviors, we have been programmed by our families to relate to others and to the world in a fearful and narrow way. Most of us act like little children still seeking parental approval. Playing it safe, protecting your heart, fearful of being rejected, of being vulnerable, how can you know love? In a lecture given near the end of his life, Henri Nouwen observed that if we are unable to love ourselves we cannot truly love others, because we *need* things from them, such as approval, validation, specific responses and reactions, etc. In our experience, many people remain dependent in the same ways in which they were as children.

Consider the couple celebrating their fiftieth anniversary. On what should be a joyous occasion, they criticize each other mercilessly and bicker about every detail. They are obviously miserable together. Is the mere fact that they have endured one another for fifty years a cause for celebration? They have had the same destructive conversation for fifty years, pecking at each other like two crows. Their celebration is a charade. If they could have life-affirming, "lived" experiences instead of celebrating what is destructive or dead, their disagreements would be seen as trivial.

Just what is a lived experience in context of another person? In relationships, a lived experience finds us present and engaged. We are open, vulnerable, and willing to risk exposure. C. S. Lewis emphasizes that there is no joy or happiness without the risk of loss or pain. It takes guts to live without fearing the disapproval of others. It is unknown territory. You are invited to explore it as you accompany us on a journey to living fully in a relationship. Most people who pick up this book are presently stuck in a prison of their past programming. We will provide some tools and direction for escape into the present, but we can't do the walking for you.

All too often, we have seen partners become very excited about spiritual concepts and believe that they can become instantaneously, unconditionally loving, and achieve immediate acceptance of themselves and others. Perhaps there are some rare souls capable of such a quick transformation, but this has not been our experience. We advise couples to be realistic about the gravitational pull back down the mountainside and into the valley. Since as human beings we don't seem capable of "unconditional love," or pure acceptance, we advise couples to use these ideas as goals while being always ready to assist each other when one starts to fall backward.

In this book, we combine the practical and the mystical to provide a map for a happy, long-term relationship. We have taken this journey in our professional work with hundreds of couples, and have chased our own tigers together as a married couple. You'll have to trust that we won't lead you down blind alleys, into dead-end relationships. To establish that trust, we'll start by telling you something about us and about our relationship.

Our own marriage has worked this way. Many times we have been profoundly grateful for each other's assistance when one of us has slid back down love's mountain. Sometimes issues from deep in our childhood have resurfaced and we both take a tumble down the mountainside; however, we have become increasingly skillful at identifying these issues and getting a hold on them quickly, before real damage is done.

For example, when we first got together, we visited Europe and took a trip on a water taxi. The water made Linda seasick. Robert didn't know her well enough to know that she got seasick. In order to cope with it, Linda tried to stare straight ahead and not look around because she felt any eye movement would make her throw up. Apparently, the boatman was staring right back at her. When they got off the boat, Robert was furious and Linda had no idea why. It took him a day to tell her what he was so mad about. He said it was humiliating to him that she would flirt with the boatman.

Robert didn't know Linda well, and he was sure she was staring at the boatman, and he felt humiliated. "At the time," he says, "I was embarrassed to tell her that it bothered me that much. It was a Catch-22. Either way, I couldn't resolve it because I was ashamed of being jealous. Now, it would be much easier to say, 'I thought you were looking at this guy, and I got very upset about it.' Of course, now I know that Linda stares straight ahead because of her seasickness, but I didn't know it then. Now we know each other well enough to be vulnerable. I could tell her now if I was feeling jealous about something. Because of my growth and the growth of the marriage there is also a much higher level of trust."

Before you get close it's difficult to deal with issues like this, but you have to, one way or another. Of course, it's best just to simply say what you're feeling. Part of doing that is making an "I" statement, and not being accusatory about it. Perhaps what Robert could have said was, "You know, I was beginning to feel jealous, and perhaps I was misunderstanding what you were doing, but I thought you were looking at that guy, and I feel embarrassed about it."

If you grow from them, negative experiences can reinforce a relationship. Think of the lessons you have to learn in life. A child learns to grasp a knife by the handle and not the blade. If you get a handle on yourself, you can start to learn to relate with another person and grow together. There will always be negative issues. From John Gottman's research at the University of Washington, we know that what separates happy couples from unhappy couples is not whether they have problems, but how they approach them.

Even broken trust can be mended, if only there is a real commitment to change behavior. For example, we've seen people who, having had affairs, successfully repaired the damage and went on to have really good marriages. We've seen other people who could never repair it. The difference seems to lie in both people really making a commitment to each other and to being present in their marriage. If one person is having a trust problem, and is emotionally distressed because they don't know where their partner is, it's important that the partner not evade them and make sure that that person knows how to reach them. They hear their partner's emotional distress and they do something about it. Over time, that's healing. We also find that if someone's had an affair, and his or her partner stonewalls and doesn't communicate, it doesn't go as well.

When she was nearly done working on this book, Linda had a power-ful near-death experience. She had developed pneumonia, and was hospitalized in critical condition for ten days. On the fourth day, she was in a crisis, all signs indicating that she was close to dying. As a physician, Robert felt helpless and distraught. As Linda felt that she was beginning to leave her body, she felt a profound sense of *knowing* what her life had been about. The only question she felt truly mattered was: "How much have I loved?" Although this had previously been an intellectual awareness, she was now certain that love is what we are accountable for in the next life.

———◆◆◆———

As a psychiatrist with over thirty years of experience in the field, Robert W. Miles, M.D. has worked in numerous areas of psychiatry, in private practice with children, adults, and families, and as an administrative phy-sician. He has a special interest in couples work and has practiced couples psychotherapy in tandem with his wife, Linda.

Linda Miles, Ph.D. has worked in the field of mental health for over twenty-five years, specializing in marriage and family work. She is cur-rently in private practice and provides consultation for organizations in the area of communication skills.

Together, we believe that it is very important to have "lived the ques-tions" about how to make a relationship work and we share many of our personal experiences in this book. We have three sons, Bobby, Blake, and Brett, and three grandchildren, Merritt, Drew, and Bobby. We live, love, and practice in Tallahassee, Florida.

It is also good to love: because love is difficult. For one human being to love another human being: that is perhaps the most difficult task that has been entrusted to us, the ultimate task, the final test and proof, the work for which all other work is merely preparation.

Rainer Maria Rilke, *Letters to a Young Poet*

Prologue

―――◦❤❤◦―――

If life is a journey across uncertain terrain, love is the mountain commanding the landscape. When you scale that mountain and survey the area, everything falls into place, and everything makes sense. You can see forever, and it all seems so simple. "Why did it take so long to get here?" you wonder.

From ground level, if you can even see the peak, obscured as it so often is by unsuitable weather and intervening hills, scaling love's heights may seem an impossible task. Some people never set foot on the path; others fall by the wayside after encountering an obstacle or two. Still others settle for temporary respite, lured by the attractions of oases in an immense, empty desert. There is much to be said for the comfort afforded by casual relationships, but a watering hole cannot sustain life indefinitely, and sometimes what seemed an oasis turns out to be just a mirage.

No doubt there are many false starts, detours, and dead ends on life's journey. There are pitfalls and jungles where fearsome beasts lie in wait, but there are also magnificent gardens where the sweet fruits of success, family, friends, good feelings and well-being proliferate. One can live and do well in such places, but life without true love and deep intimacy leaves one feeling somehow unfulfilled, somehow cheated.

We start with the premise that you are worthy of love and then differentiate true love from *faux* love. We'll test you to make sure you're not fooling yourself or your partner. Once you know who you are and what love is, you can pursue intimacy. Case studies and self-quizzes will help you make good choices and alert you to possible hazards. We'll next explore how to nurture love, protect and strengthen it, and make it last.

Problems and possible solutions will be explored in question-and-answer format, with resources suggested for specific situations.

The terrain may be rocky, but your age, gender, or sexual preference shouldn't be obstacles. It helps if your heart has already been broken. Fixing a broken heart is easier than setting out on a journey blindfolded by inexperience.

Because so many of our committed relationships are based on childhood expectations, we have little idea of what it takes to maintain a successful adult relationship. After experiencing the heights of early romantic love, most of us are ready to call it quits when faced with the rigors of daily living. We are unprepared for the journey it takes to reach lasting love. For those of us who believe in fairy tales, this new terrain is foreign and un-mapped. No one has shown us how to traverse it, or given us directions on how to get there.

Through the ages there have been couples who, despite cultural barriers, have maintained a lived experience in their marriages. How have they accomplished this? Carl Jung believed that there is great wisdom in spiritual traditions, literature, and mythology. Most fortunate couples throughout the ages, who have learned to live according to these deeper truths, beat the odds. It has become clear to us through our own personal and professional experiences that there are some universal truths that provide a model for fulfilling relationships, regardless of programmed learning from childhood or cultural limitations. These truths transcend culture and our own limited egos.

When one or both members of a couple get in touch with the "dead-ness" of the relationship, we think this is an encouraging beginning. Recognizing that you are living on automatic is essential to ending the program. Often, your partner feels the same way but is not yet in touch with this. To experience a richer, more loving life, you need to open your-self to some deeper truths about love, but in a practical way so you can apply these principles to your marriage.

In *Mere Christianity*, C. S. Lewis wrote that the principles that Jesus taught have practical applications, because when we follow the direc-tions, our lives work. When we follow our cultural or childhood programming to pursue power and money, this almost invariably lets us down. A plaque on our wall reads, "There is only one happiness—to love and be loved." (George Sand)

We have also drawn on the wisdom of poets, particularly William Blake, in exploring love's terrain. From the innocence of childhood through the valley of experience, we encounter much to inspire as well as impede our journey. In the valley of experience, as young adults, we are tempted to surrender our souls for money, security, or power. Many couples succumb and live in fancy houses and soulless marriages.

According to Pema Chodron, "There is a fundamental happiness available to every one of us—yet we miss it while spending our lives trying to escape the suffering that is quite inescapable."

As Carol Pearson says in *Awakening the Heroes*, "...the real battle is always against the enemies within—sloth, cynicism, despair, irresponsibility, denial." If we give in to these, if we refuse to discuss our feelings or face our fears, then we arrest our spiritual development and sacrifice our chance of a real relationship with another human being. Better by far to face the secrets of our own and our partner's souls no matter how ugly they may appear. To do this we must create a safe environment in which we can explore our feelings and let our deeper selves unfold.

Even after you've made your journey through the valley and emerged on the other side, you'll encounter a certain adjustment period when you come to grips with your partner's faults. You might get angry about those faults. You might not be able to accept that your partner isn't the perfect person you imagined. To deal with this, another trip to the valley might be inevitable. However, once you've been there, it's not nearly as big a drop-off as before, because you have the tools to cope and you won't get stuck.

Part One

The First Mountain: Innocence

Little Lamb, who made thee?
Dost thou know who made thee?
Gave thee life, & bid thee feed
By the stream & o'er the mead;
Gave thee clothing of delight,
Softest clothing, woolly, bright:
Gave thee such a tender voice,
Making all the vales rejoice?
Little Lamb, who made thee?
Dost thou know who made thee?

Little Lamb, I'll tell thee,
Little Lamb, I'll tell thee:
He is called by thy name,
For he calls himself a Lamb.
He is meek, & he is mild;
He became a little child.

William Blake, *The Lamb*

Base Camp

———◆◆◆———

Welcome to the beginning of an exciting journey! Before you and your partner begin to ascend the First Mountain, we will provide the tools you'll need to climb that mountain together. After experiencing the rapture atop the First Mountain, you must survive the first fall into the Valley. Only then can you experience the transformation that leads to the summit of the Second Mountain.

As experienced "mountain climbers" ourselves, we will take you step by step through the terrain until you can make the journey on your own. After all, would you embark on a long trip without planning or packing the proper equipment? Then why begin a journey as important as your relationship without a map or guide to provide direction? Come and let us show you what we have learned. We will begin the ascent of the First Mountain in the foothills of your childhood, where both tools and stumbling blocks can be found.

Before beginning our climb, let's make sure we agree on the destination: loving commitment in an exclusive relationship; that is, a monogamous relationship. Since people are imperfect, they will make mistakes. They will be tempted, and they may succumb. Committed relationships can survive indiscretions, infidelity, and other lapses. We can learn from mistakes and strengthen our resolve, but only if we value our commitment to one partner. But should we? Has monogamy outlived its usefulness? Is it still relevant? Unless you value a commitment to one person at a time, why bother to work on problems? Why not skip the hassle and take up with someone else?

We believe in monogamy because the deepening feelings promote the soul's evolution and because it's essential for strong families and civilized society. We live in a disposable culture where little has intrinsic value, but people are not disposable and enduring relationships lend meaning to life. We imbibe our belief in singular relationships with mother's milk, so let's start our journey by exploring that first experience in relating.

I'm nobody! Who are you?
Are you nobody, too?
Then there's a pair of us?—don't tell!
They'd banish us, you know.

How dreary to be somebody!
How public, like a frog
To tell your name the livelong day
To an admiring Bog!

Emily Dickinson

Chapter One:

First Love

———◈◈◈———

In the best of worlds, our parents provided for all our needs. They were great role models; they didn't smoke, drink, gamble, or fool around. Moderate in belief and temperament, they established clear, consistent, sensible rules and boundaries. We knew what to expect. They were affectionate with us and with one another. We were praised when we acted appropriately and loved no matter what we did. The consequences we suffered for our mistakes taught us right from wrong. We were held in esteem, and internalized that regard. We learned to treat others the way we wanted to be treated, and we felt compassion for those who were less well off. We had good friends from good families and attended good schools.

In this best of worlds, protected and nurtured and loved unconditionally, we would understand love intuitively. As we matured, we would choose suitable partners and in the fullness of time marry and raise children as well adjusted as we were, and live happily ever after.

Few studies have been done of couples who lived happily ever after, so we don't know how many there are, if there are any, or whether their numbers are increasing or declining; however, we suspect such couples are few and far between. Most of us had well-intentioned parents who did the best they could given the inadequacies of their own parents. Life isn't fair and then you die.

A friend we hadn't seen in many years visited us recently. Ralph was a world traveler, a well-respected photojournalist in his late forties with a knack for language acquisition. Handsome, charming, and highly paid, Ralph was envied by many of his friends despite his having been married and divorced a number of times. When he visited us, he was accompanied by his third or fourth wife, a beautiful and intelligent woman whose parents were of European nobility. We were happy for him and assumed he was happy, too. When we told him so, he responded, "How can you say that? You're both therapists; you knew my mother."

Later, we tried to conjure up an image of Ralph's mother, but all we could recall was a middle-aged housewife who was always baking something. If she was a terror, she hid it well, at least as far as was impressed upon our youthful minds.

Ralph had been in therapy for years, but he was still miserable and determined to make his wives as miserable as he was. Despite his good looks, he reminded us of Woody Allen, perpetual analysand, who would not know what to do without his neuroses.

"Your mother has been dead for more than a decade," we told him. "Get on with your life." He was unwilling to make a psychological separation from his mother. He continued to remember her as a huge witch. In our practice we suggest that clients might be able to disempower their parents if they imagine what life was like for their mother or father at four years old. Many parents are prisoners of their own childhood. It was evidently not what he wanted to hear, for he left soon thereafter and we have not seen him since, though we did learn he has divorced and remarried.

We don't mean to imply that experiences in early childhood do not define and color our future relationships, but that they can and often must be overcome if we hope to have satisfactory relationships. This can be a frightening process. People will do anything to avoid facing the fears from the past. Ralph chooses the pain and loss of divorce rather than turning to confront the witch image that haunts him. Ralph believes that it is easier to run than to own his deepest fears. He continues to blame other women for his unhappiness just as he blamed his mother. His nightmare will continue to stalk him until he turns and faces the fearful images.

Relationships might be compared to a tropical jungle that is lush and exciting as well as perilous and frightening. The powerful forces are part of a natural environment that can be understood and accepted. The tiger symbolizes these forces. Exciting, beautiful and powerful, if ignored, it can be destructive. Just as tigers prefer to sneak up from behind their prey to attack, these forces are most dangerous when your back is turned to them.

Even to this day, people are killed and consumed by tigers in the jungles of India and Pakistan. To protect themselves, they tie masks to the back of their heads to give a stalking tiger the impression that they are watching it from behind. Since tigers prefer to stalk the unaware, the knowing eyes looking back at them discourage an attack. In like manner, if we are aware of and take responsibility for facing tigers from our childhood, they are far less likely to consume us.

How We Learn and Think as Children

Bright couples are so subtle and creative at pushing each other away because of their fears. They disguise what they're doing by using intellectual language, a detached, disinterested voice, a low-key sermon or a professional demeanor.

When we fail to get the response or connection with our partner that we want, perhaps we should stop and look at our own thoughts and behavior. It may remind us of frightful tigers from our past stalking the room. Sometimes a calm and collected exterior hides demons lingering from childhood. But how do we uncover the real person underneath our sophisticated facade? We climbed that mountain so long ago; the path we took may be lost in the undergrowth.

Our ascent of the First Mountain begins at birth. The learning we undergo in our early childhood is intense and shapes our experiences of love and adolescence when we are further up the mountainside. The ways in which we perceived things as children affected our neurological connections and influenced our later behavior in relationships. Modern research on the brain has revealed how critical early learning affects the way we behave with and perceive the partner of our mature years.

Very early in our careers a couple came to see us who had been arguing for the last year over where to store the dishes in their kitchen. Each held a Ph.D. and both were academics—yet they were completely unable to solve this problem.

We made the mistake of trying to help them at a concrete level, when obviously if the problem was practical two such clever people could have readily dealt with it themselves. We then realized that their problem had to do with the learning they had brought with them from their childhood. Each family household had been managed in different ways and they felt disloyal to their family of origin if they diverged from what they'd learned, since internalizing the family's patterns of behavior is a child's way of feeling he or she belongs. Once this internalization has happened, questioning the behavior, even in adulthood, can cause anxiety about one's identity and self-worth. The couple was at odds because of behavior they each had internalized many years before their marriage.

This realization was important in our journeys as psychotherapists. We started to look more deeply for answers as to why couples maintain destructive interactions—interactions that seemed so obviously pointless and damaging. There were still many questions: Why, after all, did all the learning and intelligence these two academics had acquired since childhood appear to count for nothing in their relationship? Why was the learned behavior of their childhood so pervasive in their personal lives and so absent from their professional ones? Why was there this division? We began to do some research...

We found the confirmation we were looking for in the concept of "attachment style."

Attachment Style

Harry Stack Sullivan, in *The Interpersonal Theory of Psychiatry*, argues that human beings have a biological drive to develop and establish interpersonal relationships. In *Biological Basis for Human Social Behavior*, R.A. Hind suggests that a person's "attachment style"—the way in which they relate to other human beings and form relationships with them—is developed mostly during childhood. The attachment style tends to persist into adulthood but is not fixed and can be modified either positively or negatively as the result of further interactions.

We have had the joy of seeing countless adult clients consciously change their attachment style. This is a practice that takes time and is not easy to do. However, we have seen many people move from a victim stance to living more fully by changing their attachment style.

Helen was a lovely, dark-haired young woman, the adult child of an alcoholic. Her attachment style led her to be attracted to what she called "bad boys." Helen told us she "had radar for the bad boys in the room," those who would treat her with indifference and ultimately disappoint her. She had been married for five years to Paul, who was extremely critical of her, had multiple affairs, and was also an alcoholic.

We worked hard on her attachment style. Like many clients, she could not trust her unconscious processes to choose an appropriate partner. We had her make a list of the characteristics that she was looking for in a partner and had her carry it around with her in her wallet. One bright November morning she came in to tell us of her triumph with another bad boy situation.

"I was consciously able to make a choice to not follow my attraction," Helen explained. "I was at a party and was approached by a very attractive and charming man. My radar went up immediately, because I felt a strong attraction to his good looks and charm. However, I also started looking for indications that he was the type of man that I had been attracted to in the past. I did not have to consider this for very long because I realized that he had a date who was over getting something for both of them to drink. I decided on the spot that I did not want to go out with him when he asked me out on a date, when he already had a date." So began a real change in Helen's attachment style. She has since married a conscientious, devoted husband.

An attachment style is not simply made up of behavior we have learned at our parents' knees. An attachment style is a way of thinking and feeling as well, and shapes not just what we do, but the meaning we give to the things that happen between our partner and ourselves. The way we think as children can persist into our adult lives.

Despite the learning we do later that develops rational thinking and professional skills, there is a tendency to hold onto child-like ways of thinking in our long-term and intimate relationships. Our professional skills are things we learn as adults, but as H. Stadtman Main points out, love and attachment we learn as children.

We think of the period when the child is learning about love as the individual's beginning of the journey that will lead him or her to the heights of rapturous love and then, all too frequently, into the valley of faultfinding and blame-gaming. One's attachment style lays the groundwork. Foster parents frequently report the lengths to which an abused or neglected child will go to protect and defend their birth parents, frequently blaming themselves rather than the abusive parent. Also well documented is the "cycle of abuse," whereby abused children become abusive parents. Such behavior patterns are difficult to break, no matter that after each episode the abuser is remorseful and promises never to do it again.

The work of Harry Stack Sullivan and others has many implications for couples. While it identifies the existence of pre-formed attachment styles as a possible cause of interpersonal difficulties, it also contends that problematic attachment styles can be addressed and changed. We'll have a lot more to say about change in the second part of this book. Here we want to concentrate on the psychology of the child and how internalized behavior affects later relationships.

Who Am I?

When we are children we do not yet have an identity. We learn about who we are through the mirroring that we get from our parents. It is called mirroring to describe the ability of good parents to gently hold up an imaginary mirror in front of the child until they learn to see themselves clearly without harsh judgments. If we do not get enough realistic mirroring during the years we live with them, we remain pretty clueless about who we really are.

We are always so pleased to see parents who appropriately mirror their children. By providing them feedback about their behavior without shame or blame, parents help children grow up with a realistic self-image and the ability to operate from a strong sense of self.

In our children's book, *Amanda Salamander*, written with Martin Terrell, we tell the story of a beautiful young salamander who changes herself into the color of whomever she is with so that they will like her. This is quite characteristic of what we learn to do when we do not have a good picture of who we are. In the story, Amanda Salamander turns into the color of her husband so that he will like her. This brings many problems into their marriage, because she is not being true to herself.

We wrote *Amanda Salamander* to advise children of the perils of entering a relationship by pretending to be someone else. When we read this story to our five-year-old granddaughter, she already understood what we were talking about. We asked her what the lesson was in this story and she responded, "You should stay your same color when you get married." However, we first need to know what our true color is!

An example of a parent doing a good job of mirroring a sense of self to her children without shame and blame occurred one day when we took a picture of a group of neighborhood children. Except for one four-year-old girl we'll call Lillith, all the children were boys. Lillith wanted to be in the middle of the picture, and when the boys refused, she began to whine. It's not hard to guess the reaction of young boys to a whining girl. This behavior was obviously not in her best interest.

Lillith's mother wisely called her over to the side and knelt down to her level. She explained, "Lillith, you know that thing you do that causes you problems? You are doing it right now." What this woman was doing so naturally was mirroring back behavior that was not in the child's best interest without sounding overly judgmental. Therefore, she was helping Lillith to begin to look at her own behavior and to self-correct. Consequently, Lillith pushed herself into the middle of the boys and they seemed to respect this behavior and allowed her to get her picture taken. Ultimately, that is not the behavior that we would want to encourage. Lillith, however, is beginning to experiment with something different based on her mother's mirroring.

Sadly, we have seen countless adults who really do not have a sense of who they are. We were present when one woman realized that when her husband had asked her to marry him, all she had thought about was whether he would want to marry her. She had never even asked herself whether she might want to marry him.

The clinical term for the development of a self is *differentiation*. Developed by a brilliant family therapist named Murray Bowen, this concept refers to our ability to be close to others and also maintain a sense of self. This is perhaps the most difficult task that we have in our lives.

It requires a great deal of learning and trial and error to begin to figure out who we are. We are not doomed if we do not develop an accurate mirror as children. This can be developed through our relationships as adults.

All or Nothing

Children's limited experience of life makes them believe that their parents are always good and that adults can always be trusted. Carried over into adult life and love, this way of thinking forms the psychology of the first summit—the first period of our involvement with another when love is experienced as rapturous. Our new partner seems faultless, good in every way.

Terri had felt unloved all her life. When she began a relationship with a man who doted on her and always wanted to be by her side, she thought she had found the "perfect man." But, it didn't last. Gradually, she realized that Andrew was an alcoholic who had no life of his own apart from the excitement he found in starting a new relationship. Terri's experience was the product of her childhood tendency to think in "all or nothing" terms.

The pattern of Terri's romance is one we have seen repeated many times. Excited clients come in at the beginning of a relationship and tell us that they have found the "perfect person." Unfortunately, disappointment awaits them. When it comes, they fall off the rapturous summit of first love and tumble down into the valley. The partner who was "all-perfect" becomes "all-bad" and worth "nothing."

Neither view is very realistic. If you want to build a relationship that will last, you'll have to come to grips with the humanity and failings of your intimate partner. Surrendering the "all or nothing" ideal is a necessary loss, but what you can gain is so much more. We know. We did not give up easily on fairy tales ourselves. But we have learned that relating to the complexity of another human being is ultimately more satisfying than squashing them into an "all good" or "all bad" mold. At the same time, it is the sign of a healthy relationship if a couple has managed to retain some of the excitement and interest in each other that was there at the beginning. We keep contact both with the idealism of rapturous love and with reality by referring to each other as "imperfectly perfect"!

Some people are so locked into themselves that they're oblivious of everything outside. It's as if they put a paper bag over their heads when they venture into society. They stumble about in an all-or-nothing way until they bump into someone who arouses their passion. Tearing the bag from their heads, they are struck with light, color, and beauty. They gaze into one another's eyes and utter the magic words, "I love you."

For a while, bliss takes them to places of unimagined loveliness, but reality soon intrudes, as in the case of the couple who couldn't agree on where to store their dishes. It may be as simple a defining moment as the failure to replace the cap on a tube of toothpaste, or as complicated as relating to a lover's children from a previous marriage, but without a grounding in self-awareness, coming to terms with someone else can be frighteningly formidable. One must by any means protect oneself. At first, unconscious lovers close their eyes and hope it will all go away. When this doesn't work, the partner is blamed for pretending to be everything when they were really nothing at all. And so, the paper bag is unfolded, smoothed out and put on. The world is monochromatic once more, but the pain is diffused along with the light. There's no need to feel sorry for such people. They will love again. And again. And again. They will believe in the "happily ever after" myth at the expense of genuine (if more complex) relationships and go on singing "Someday my prince will come," the sound muffled by the bag they wear over their heads.

In *The Screwtape Letters*, C. S. Lewis suggests several other ways we might be led astray by what we think is love. Familiarity is one way: "When two humans have lived together for many years, it usually happens that each has tones of voice and expressions of face that are almost unendurably irritating to the other. Work on that," Screwtape advises his nephew Wormwood, an apprentice demon. Lewis refers to "peak" and "trough" experiences rather than "mountain" and "valley" experiences, but the terrain is the same: "Trough sexuality is subtly different in quality from that of the Peak—much less likely to lead to the milk-and-water phenomenon which the humans call 'being in love,' much more easily drawn into perversions..." To Lewis, one such perversion is promiscuity, which has gained favor, Screwtape is pleased to report: "We have done this through the poets and novelists by persuading the humans that a curious, and usually short-lived, experience which they call 'being in love' is the only respectable ground for marriage; that marriage can, and ought to, render this excitement permanent; and that a marriage which does not do so is no longer binding."

Many people have trouble relating because they're so wrapped up in their own lives they're unable to perceive or understand their partners' needs or desires. Nothing epitomizes this better than the beliefs and attitudes displayed by some members of the "me generation" of the '80s.

It's All About Me

A characteristic of childhood thinking is the child's assumption that whatever happens "is all about me." The tendency of children to blame themselves for their parents' difficulties causes them great pain, and if this kind of "it's all about me" thinking persists into adulthood, it can do considerable harm to their personal relationships. As adults, many people still believe they are defective and that if people really knew them they would be rejected.

Children under the age of ten have yet to develop a concept of multi-causality. Consequently, they explain out-of-the-ordinary phenomena as having occurred because they made them happen. Young children do not see their overly critical parents for what they are—overly critical. As children they cannot understand that their parents might have, let us say, a drinking problem, which distorts their personalities and behavior. Rather, children believe that if they are criticized it must be because they really are bad and the proper cause of all the criticism that comes their way. Similarly, if things start to go wrong between parents, children think they are the reason or that they can provide the solution.

Several clients have brought home to us how extreme the discrepancy can be between the logic of the adult and the emotions of the inner child. In one case, Mary, a bright and attractive professional woman was trying to deal with a relationship breakup. She explained, "I really don't know why I am so upset. This relationship had to end since he couldn't get along with my daughter. He'd made it clear that he did not want to raise another child and since my child is only six he was unable to commit…so why am I devastated?"

We could have tried to assist Mary by strengthening her resolve, but she didn't really need us for that. She was perfectly capable of coming up with every logical, rational reason under the sun why the relationship wasn't viable and was best ended. She had intelligent friends to assist her with that, too.

Our job was to redirect Mary to her childhood. Her own father had left the family when she was six. Using the child's "it's all about me" way of thinking, she had decided that if only she had been good enough, or worthwhile enough, her father would not have left. Her goodness would have made him stay. She felt the same way about her breakup with her boyfriend and was re-traumatized by it. Indicatively, she told us that there was a part of her that wanted to try to make the relationship work at any price, so that this time it would be different, even though she could see with her adult mind that the relationship was not really a good one. She didn't even know the man that well. Talking it through, she became able to see that most of the feelings she had about her partner were a projection from the past and not based on reality.

When the final break came, Mary was able to be caring and not caustic or blaming toward him. She said, "I know that he is a good person and means well and has always been honest with me." Saying this was progress for her, because in past relationships she tended to get angry with her partner and blame him for everything that went wrong between them. She had begun to make sense of the strength of her feelings, and her adult and child were more integrated. Working through the stages of the relationship without reverting to blaming her partner gave her an opportunity to deal with the pain in her past, understand herself more deeply, and become more conscious in relationships.

We have seen many individuals who believed that their partner's bad behavior was their fault, thus taking responsibility for someone else's destructive behaviors. One client told us that she had "caused" her husband to break her leg during a beating by saying something provocative to him. We attempted to explain to her that her partner's assaultive behavior was illegal, but to no avail. She persisted in believing that she was the "cause" of her partner's physical attacks on her.

In our marriage, we have to be attentive to the tendency we both have to feel overly responsible for things. We usually have to work on getting our signals straight when one or the other of us is in a bad mood and withdrawing. We try to head off the possibility of the other feeling blamed or guilty by saying to each other things like: "I have had a really bad day and I feel like I need to withdraw, but it has nothing to do with you." We find this kind of proactive measure very useful.

Magical Thinking

Expressed as a two-way bridge between childhood and adulthood, magical thinking is a developmental stage during childhood that serves a very important function in the process of creativity and imagination. Like so many of our developmental constructs, when magical thinking is held onto and not revised in the light of reality it becomes maladaptive.

The Perfect Other

Many of our illusions about relationships are childhood fairy tales exported into adulthood fairy tales in the form of myths about relationships. The myth of the "perfect other," usually represented in fairy tales by the prince or the princess, sends many dreamers on a lifelong path of searching and rejecting serial candidates. The rapturous "falling in love" stage of relationship leads them to believe in the possibility of perpetual bliss with a perfect other. They believe they can sustain this rapture if only they could find that perfect partner. This is the fodder of romantic novels, music and singles bars and other partner-seeking activities. Sadly, most of these efforts lead us on a false trail.

When Harry met Phyllis, Fleetwood Mac was singing "You'll Never Break the Chain," and they took the lyrics to heart: "If you don't love me now, you will never love me again." They swore they'd never break the chain of love, and for several months they succeeded in stuffing anything that threatened their love. The tension was palpable when they came to see us, and when we encouraged them to talk about what disturbed them, a litany of complaints overwhelmed the levies they had erected to protect their relationship. Once that was out of the way, however, they could begin to relate to the real person beneath the perfect mask each was trying to wear.

The Pygmalion Dynamic

Another variation of the perfect other myth is the belief that one partner can change the other into his or her perfect person. Believing that you can change your partner to fit your ideal image of what the perfect partner should be creates an unbalanced relationship. In *My Fair Lady*, adapted from George Bernard Shaw's play based on the Pygmalion myth, an ill-bred Eliza Doolittle is transformed into a cultured lady through the efforts of Mr. Higgins, who places a bet on his ability to perform social magic. Whether or not the experiment is successful, one person is constantly "under construction" and being made over, while the other is constantly kneading and shaping their partner. This tug of war can become a lifetime struggle that ultimately leads to disappointment, stalemate, affairs, and divorce. We suggest that people never marry "potential."

Although you can change many aspects of yourself if you really want to, attempts to change your partner are rarely successful and even more rarely appreciated. You'll more likely encounter resistance, intransigence, and resentment despite your best intentions. In an egalitarian relationship, both partners respect one another and offer support and encouragement when the other partner decides to alter his or her behavior, appearance, or lifestyle.

Image: The Bridge of Magical Thinking

The Reverse Pygmalion Dynamic—Projective Identification

Closely related to the perfect other myth is the practice of casting your partner in a role from the drama of your past. When you choose a partner who resembles a former caretaker, you may be attempting to work out developmental issues with an adult partner to heal your childhood wounds. Sometimes, instead of selecting a partner with your unresolved childhood issues in an attempt to "fix" that person, you can turn a partner without those characteristics into one who manifests them.

Joyce, a professional librarian, had an untrustworthy and unreliable father who would lie to the family about most matters. Having had such an untrustworthy model as a father, Joyce had incorporated that view of men into her relationship with her husband, Jessup. Based on his developmental history and adult relationships, Jessup did not appear to have such characteristics. However, after Joyce subjected him to interrogation, scrutiny and painful consequences for being forthright, Jessup began to lie and withhold information from her. For example, he would lie about going to see friends because of fear of her reaction and would say he was going to the grocery. When she caught him she would call him a "liar."

In this manner, Joyce was able to "prove" that she was right about men after all, and her prophecy became self-fulfilling. Jessup had in fact begun lying to her about many matters. She had unconsciously and unintentionally reconstructed her childhood issues to play out in the context of her marriage. Our tendency to incongruously set up our partners to play certain roles is often more difficult to recognize and correct than the selection of a partner who resembles a parent. For your journey to be successful it is important to realize that the child of the past lives on in you, as it does in all of us. Acknowledge that child and be aware of its manifestations in your adult life and relationships.

It is well known that when abused children are removed from their parents, within a short period of time they will provoke violent impulses in even the most "saintly" caretakers. We have found it remarkable on many occasions to see partners playing out the script of the other person's family drama. Current literature emphasizes the tendency to pick someone who resembles our caretakers. Frequently this is not our experience. For example, if you asked objective raters to pick a person most likely to lie, Jessup would not be chosen. As a matter of fact, he was also in group therapy with us and had a tendency to be so honest that tact was a problem! Repeatedly we have observed that people may be very different in an individual session than they are with their partner. We have learned that couples teach the other how to treat them.

In the movie *Alien*, starring Sigourney Weaver, creatures are implanted in a host person that later explode from the body. The host body dies, leaving a threatening alien. In similar fashion, we implant embryonic entities from our unconscious fears of the past that later hatch into frightful aliens. Our partner plays the host in which we implant the alien. Before us stands our deepest dread. We remain unaware of our part in creating this nightmare. Couples find it helpful when they are able to own their own fears and projections. They stop seeing the other person as an alien and realize he or she is a complex human being who has played out a part in a mutual creature feature. The clinical term "projective identification" refers to the tendency to project our unfinished business from the past onto someone else. We have found this process to greatly influence couples. We do not think it has been given enough attention in the literature. Much has been said about the tendency to repeat patterns from childhood and to chose partners with similar characteristics. More consideration needs to be given to the part the individual plays in recreating the drama from the past.

You can minimize the valley experience by recognizing your tigers and your projections, because they're what get you stuck. When you project your stuff onto your partners, all that limbic snake brain stuff, and your reactions to it, can get out of hand. That's when the tigers come out of the trees to pounce on you. The valley and its shadows become very powerful then, because the fears are unconscious and from your past. Reliving those experiences is what makes them so powerful.

Mind Reading

When Ann came to see us, she was in the process of counting how many times in the past year her husband had turned on the television when she wanted to talk to him—not that she had ever told him she wanted to talk. She left him oblivious to her upset, while her resentment built at his failure to magically "know" what was on her mind.

When we are young it seems as if our caretakers magically know when we need to eat and what they must do to take care of us. Children have a family romance in which their parents are always wise and good. This is extended to the whole world via the culture of children's stories, in which wonderful things happen to the good guys and the bad guys get their due. The Prince comes. The slipper fits. They live happily ever after.

In adulthood this can become the expectation: that our partners should always know what we need without our having to tell them. When our partner fails to read our minds and to "magically" know our needs, resentment builds. We can take our partner's "blindness" as a criticism of what we want or as a failure to do their part in the relationship. We have seen many couples who both believe that the other one knows, "just knows," what it is they need and is withholding it for reasons of perversity or vindictiveness. This leads to a kind of passivity and watching in the relationship. We wait and wait for our partner to recognize us by doing for us the thing we feel they should know to do. We describe this as "saving brown stamps." Meanwhile, resentment builds and we cease to be a proper participant in the relationship.

Our belief that there is a force outside of our lives magically steering it toward love and happiness is deeply ingrained; usually it is only given up as a consequence of repeated disappointments. Even when it is, we can still become involved in trying to be the perfect person ourselves, believing that our slimness or muscularity will exercise a magical attraction on others around us. Thus women become anorexic and men spend hours at the gym. These behaviors often represent an attempt to keep our belief in magic alive.

Dependency/Fear of Abandonment

Rebecca, who had been separated from her husband for two years, felt hopelessly abandoned, yet she was a highly intelligent and capable person. While still with her husband, she had functioned quite independently of him much of the time. We told her we did not feel it would benefit her if we reinforced the idea that she was a victim. When her husband was very clear about wanting a divorce she was distraught, but once the divorce became a reality she adapted to it and flourished. In our practice we have seen many people become so distressed about losing their partners that they may threaten or even attempt suicide out of a desperate desire to hold onto their partner's attention. They do not believe they can survive without their partners.

It is quite normal for a child to feel and be dependent. A young child would not survive without its parents, and it is only to be expected that he or she will have fears about separation from them. However, these kinds of separation anxieties can persist into adulthood and create an unhealthy level of dependency in our intimate relationships.

When Rebecca was in her twenties, she still had fears about being left at home alone, and was largely dependent on her peers and significant others for feelings of self-worth. We have seen many people who damage their relationships through fear of their partner doing things without them, like taking a trip with other friends, or joining an organization they are not part of. Fear of abandonment makes them try to control their partner's activities. Although intellectually they know that they can survive and make their way in the world, they feel that they still need someone to take care of them emotionally.

Sibling Rivalry

It is not unusual for a client to say, "You will like my husband better than me," or, "Everyone likes my wife and not me." We also see rivalry between mothers and daughters for the father's attention, and between fathers and sons for the mother's. In these cases people conceive of one another as siblings with whom they are in competition.

All siblings vie with each other for the attention of their parents, and believe that if they are "perfect" their parents will love them more than the rest. Sometimes they believe that one of their brothers or sisters is the perfect child and that they can never compete—a feeling younger children are particularly prone to.

Carried over into adult relationships, a sense of competing with, or for, one's partner is usually not helpful. Research suggests that successful families encourage accommodation—try to meet everyone's needs—rather than encouraging or rewarding competition.

The net result of the child's ways of thinking is that by the time a person reaches adulthood, a conviction may be in place that he or she is fundamentally defective. Many children of broken homes believe their parents divorced because they did something to cause it, or weren't "worth" staying together for. A lack of parental attention can establish separation fears or a poor self-image, and so on.

Whatever the specific cause, children who carry this sense of defectiveness into adulthood will have a tendency to settle for bad treatment in their relationships because deep down they believe they deserve no better. Or they believe that if they are in a relationship that is exciting and challenging, they will be revealed as frauds, and so they opt for something less satisfying.

Of the people we see, at least eighty percent have problems that are some sort of variation on this theme: they decided as children that they were defective and they have not updated the decision as adults.

In a way this is not surprising. It takes courage to face this decision and test it. It takes courage to demand better treatment or choose a more challenging partner. When you do so, questions and doubts as to your self-worth can overwhelm you.

Early in her relationship with Robert, Linda's conflict between her desire to be with Robert and her sense that she wasn't deserving of him was almost too much for her to bear. According to Linda, "I believed that if we ever lived together Robert would be sure to discover that I was defective. For several months, I felt depressed. My sense of my own unworthiness was so great I was plunged into feelings of doom about the relationship's prospects. This culminated in a stress-related illness that put me in bed for several days." Linda managed to confront her fears and pursue a plan of action.

She wrote down all the flaws that she believed made the case for how defective she was. Then she asked Robert to go to dinner because she told him, "I need to talk to you about something important." When they were finally sitting down, she went through the whole list with him.

His response was "Is that it?"

"I cannot begin to say how healing that was for me," Linda said. "Robert did not expect me to be perfect. None of the faults I thought were so grave troubled him very deeply. On the way home he played a Billy Joel song for me entitled 'I Love You Just the Way You Are.'"

Facing her doubts about herself with Robert proved "the most therapeutic thing I have done in my life."

There are so few soulful models of marriage that maintain a deep connection with the transcendent qualities of love. When you first fall in love the world is alive, wondrous, meaningful. You sparkle with the cosmic dance. In *We, Understanding the Psychology of Romantic Love*, Robert Johnson describes falling in love as an initiation into another realm, where you appreciate and worship forces that transcend your own ego. You are swept up into powers beyond your control or reasoning. This is the divine mystery of love. However, we need adult preparation for the realities in order to maintain the sparkle.

Couple Exercises

Exercise 1

Do you recall the beginning of your relationship, when you first fell in love? Describe your behavior.

Describe your partner's behavior.

Too often in a long-term relationship partners stop the very behaviors that connected them with one another and with transcendent reality. Some common examples are:

Looking deeply into one another's eyes
Concentrated attention
Compliments, gifts, etc.

What do you no longer do?
What has your partner stopped doing?
What behaviors would you like to restore to your relationship?

Exercise 2

What behaviors bother you most about your partner?

Are these issues similar to issues from your past? If so, what part do you play in implanting the negative behaviors in your partner?

How could you change your behavior to encourage a more positive response?

Part Two

The Valley Experience

Tyger! Tyger! burning bright
In the forests of the night,
What immortal hand or eye
Could frame thy fearful symmetry?

In what distant deeps or skies
Burnt the fire of thine eyes?
On what wings dare he aspire?
What the hand dare seize the fire?

And what shoulder, & what art,
Could twist the sinews of thy heart?
And when thy heart began to beat,
What dread hand? & what dread feet?

What the hammer? what the chain?
In what furnace was thy brain?
What the anvil? what dread grasp
Dare its deadly terrors clasp?

When the stars threw down their spears,
And water'd heaven with their tears,
Did he smile his work to see?
Did he who made the Lamb make thee?

Tyger! Tyger! burning bright
In the forests of the night,
What immortal hand or eye,
Dare frame thy fearful symmetry?

William Blake, *The Tyger*

Chapter Two:

Heartbreak

—◦❖◦—

The rapture of first love is a tremendously powerful experience that affects us biologically, psychologically, and spiritually. Robert Johnson writes of love in *We, Understanding the Psychology of Romantic Love,* as an initiation into a state of higher consciousness. It seems no less, but we receive this initiation at such a young age that usually we are without the life experiences that instruct us in the management of the powerful force that love is.

In the 1960s, Dr. Jerry Stern gave a lecture on the poet William Blake, explaining the importance of having a lived experience. To represent the innocent phase, Blake wrote about little lambs and the world of the child. In the experience phase, Blake shows that we must deal with our fears and "face the tigers" of life as we interact with the real world and make our inevitable mistakes. Finally, Blake uses innocence and experience to transform life and take it to the next stage, the Second Mountain, which we'll explore in Part Two. To get there, we must first traverse jungle and desert.

Relationships might be compared to a tropical jungle, lush and exciting but also perilous and frightening. The powerful forces in that jungle are neither good nor bad; they are part of a natural environment with cycles and forces that can be understood and accepted. Exciting, beautiful, and powerful, the tiger personifies those forces. If ignored, the tiger can also be destructive. Just as tigers prefer to sneak up behind their prey to attack, these forces are dangerous when your back is turned to them.

A poignant example of this is found in the jungles of India and Pakistan, where woodcutters and fishermen are regularly killed and eaten by tigers. However, the people who live there accept the environment and all it holds, harvesting the bounty of their rich land while understanding its perils. Their awareness of this dynamic is represented by an incredibly symbolic technique, described earlier: when moving through the jungle they tie masks to the back of their heads, giving a stalking tiger the impression that they are watching it from behind. As tigers prefer stalking those who are unaware of their presence, the cats will seek less threatening prey. Similarly, if we are aware of and take responsibility for facing the tigers in our own lives, they will be far less likely to pursue us.

Rapturous Love: The First Summit

The rapture phase of love gives each partner a feeling that is buoyant, lively, and fulfilling. You project onto your partner images of beauty, goodness, and love as if your partner were a canvas waiting to be painted on. The energy of this consciousness shines a bright light across the world, obliterating all the differences in your characters, lifting you and your partner to a higher state of being. You are atop the summit of the First Mountain, and you sparkle to one another like diamonds with many facets of light.

This is as it should be. Robert Johnson observed that falling in love is meant to be an initiation into a world much greater than the individual: an introduction to the ideals of love, truth, and beauty that transcend the personal ego and ordinary life.

Problems arise when we do not learn how to manage the powerful energies that are released by love, when, months or years later, couples begin to become aware of their differences and begin finding fault with each other. They fall into the valley, and the intense energy they had felt becomes soulless and rigid as they engage in "right-wrong" games. Their energies are channeled into a power struggle that can last for years as they stumble about through thickets and the "forests of the night." They lose sight of the partner they had loved so much and turn them into a threatening figure from their past—a stalking "tiger." Their potential for transcendence and a relationship that is greater than the sum of its parts is squandered, and they lose themselves in the jungle of faultfinding and blaming. If this describes your situation, before you can free yourself, you must identify the forces at work in the shadowy realm that surrounds you.

The good news is, you are no longer held fast by fairy tales, and transformation can begin. One of the most important lessons you must learn is that you cannot have transformation without experience, for it's the lived experience that allows you to create the transformation. You do not have to lose romance and passion in your relationship after giving up the fairy tales. Love gets better once you achieve transformation, and it's well worth the effort.

Into the Valley—Disappointment

In our culture, we do not prepare people for the drop-off and the disappointment that come after that first marvelous experience of rapture. Instead, we continually expose our children to fairy tales that end with the reassurance that the handsome prince and beautiful princess lived happily ever after. In substance, this is a lie. The real work is only just beginning and we do a disservice to our children by instructing them otherwise.

In its own way, the drop-off stage of a relationship is just as powerful as the rapture stage. We begin to find fault with the partner who had seemed "perfect" to us only weeks before. Our fears about what may be at stake in a relationship, i.e., being abandoned, being engulfed, being rejected, etc., begin to surface and we withdraw from or attack our partner. In this phase, the critical issue is self-acceptance. If we do not develop a comfortable relationship with ourselves, then we are in no position to develop a good relationship with others. Tigers like "the shadow" and "the critic" stalk us, powerful forces that make for discord and low self-esteem.

The lack of preparation in our culture for this difficult phase has horrendous consequences for marital life. According to Dr. Larry Barlow, president of the Florida Association of Marriage & Family Therapy, it is projected that *sixty-seven* out of every 100 people who marry in the '90s will eventually divorce. This is relational failure on a massive scale. Nor is there any room for complacency about the remaining thirty-three percent. Approximately twenty percent of them will pass the majority of their married lives in a "cold war," a state where the two people involved will have turned away from each other and given up on meeting each other's needs. The lowlands are a very dangerous place.

It doesn't take long to succumb. In fact, fifty percent of married couples divorce by the seventh year of marriage. It's painful to be rejected, but a broken heart can create fertile ground for learning who you are and preparing you for future relationships. Regardless of whether the breakup was mutual or one-sided, resist the temptation to jump into a new relationship before you've had the chance to learn all you can about the one that just ended.

On the other hand, there could still be life left in the relationship. You may be stuck in a simple disagreement with your partner, or perhaps some childhood issue has suddenly reared its head. Whatever the state, some of the "magic" has rubbed off and you find yourself at odds with one another. You might even be considering bailing out of the relationship. That's understandable. Without the proper tools and knowledge, the Valley of the Shadows is a very gloomy place indeed. Tigers lurk nearby. You may be asking, "Is it worth it?" Sadly, many don't ask; they just flee. The bones of broken marriages and aborted relationships litter the valley floor.

But hold on a minute. Before fleeing the valley, take another look at yourself and your partner and face your tigers. Remember that a tiger senses fear, so you must face it head on. Don't panic. Even though the valley may be frightening, what you can learn about yourself and about how you relate to others can guide you out and up the Mountain of Transformation. You can survive setbacks; sudden falls into the valley, and your relationship will grow stronger and richer. It's well worth the struggle. So, take a deep breath, and prepare to meet your shadow.

The Shadow

According to Carl Jung, the shadow is "the inferior part of the personality; sum of all personal and collective psychic elements which, because of their incompatibility with the chosen conscious attitude, are denied expression in life and therefore coalesce into a relatively autonomous 'splinter personality.'"

In his *Little Book on the Human Shadow*, the poet Robert Bly develops Jung's concept, describing the shadow as "the long bag we drag behind us." We put into the shadow bag all the things about ourselves that we have sensed our parents don't like and that don't fit in with their concept of a "good child."

In the Buddhist tradition, the Bodhisattva, or Compassionate One, is sometimes shown holding a mirror or a purifying flame to symbolize the belief that we can only alleviate our suffering if we are prepared to look at ourselves and shine a light within. Getting to know our shadow involves the process of holding a mirror up to ourselves, shining a light within. The process begins with accepting ourselves as flawed human beings. Then we must try to integrate the disowned parts of ourselves that were unacceptable to our caretakers or our culture. Once we do that we can begin to look at our own contributions to the problems in a relationship.

When we ask couples who have managed to turn their relationships around, what made the difference, they usually say things like: "Getting to know myself"; "Finding out that I was not a victim"; "Looking at the part I play in the destructiveness"; "Taking my own inventory instead of my partner's."

Such self-knowledge shows them moving beyond the blame-gaming phase where if something is wrong in a relationship it is always their partner's fault. When we see who we are and the contribution we make to the relationship, we also cease to see ourselves as helpless children whom the ghosts must come out to protect.

As we often tell couples, there are no "cupcakes" in a marriage or long-term relationship. A relationship is co-created by its two members. For a person to be whole and for the relationship to be whole we must be prepared to acknowledge and reclaim what are often distasteful and disorderly parts of ourselves. If we do not do this, the shadow will tend to take charge of our relationship and act outside of our awareness.

We need to be patient and non-judgmental with each other and ourselves as we work with the shadow. Learning to look without judgment at our partners and ourselves isn't easy, but it's worth the effort. The gain of turning the "ghosts" that haunt us into "ancestors" is that it leaves us greater flexibility and more energy for our present relations. We found this out when we wrestled with the two splinter personalities that haunted our marriage—Buck and Nadine.

Buck and Nadine

Buck and Nadine are a couple of characters we managed to identify when we attended a workshop given by Dr. Anthony Spoto, who is interested in the various sub-personalities that make up our identities. He suggests giving them names and then dialoguing with them. This process of personification and dialogue helps us to learn more about them and contain their influence if necessary. Buck and Nadine were two of our more troublesome ghosts before we transformed them into ancestors.

Buck is a descendent of Attila the Hun. Like any successful Hun, Buck is dominating, powerful, and operates on the assumption that "might makes right." These character traits have their origin in various important childhood experiences. Buck was taught from a young age that he should be a leader, using his intelligence, athletic abilities, and height to that end.

Buck has a deep distrust of women, due to his mother being repeatedly hospitalized with psychosis during his early childhood, and his father's second marriage to a woman only a few years older than Buck. When Buck's father died, this second wife kicked Buck out of the house, leaving him homeless at the age of fifteen. He survived by relying on his will, determination, and capacity to dominate.

Buck brings out the counterpart ghost, Nadine, who is nagging, persistent, and vengeful, and whose operating assumption is, "I'll wear you down." Although she appears pliant, Nadine is really passive-aggressive. For at least three generations, women in her family have lost husbands at a young age. They survived by nagging their children and learning to manipulate men in a man's world in which they were fundamentally powerless.

Having identified these aspects of our personalities, we always refer to them by their proper names. A sample of dialogue might sound like this:

Buck (bellowing): Who's taken my blue shirt?
Nadine (whining): Buck, do you really want this conversation? I mean, I'll be glad to give you some excuses and talk you to death, but...
Buck (no emotion): How about if we just concentrate on the shirt problem?

When Buck and Nadine are viewed with understanding, compassion, and a sense of history, they don't take over. They are turned from ghosts into ancestors who keep their place in the past. We know that both these characters are only parts of us, parts that we have named in order to know them better and control their influence upon us. But they are woven into the fabric of our personalities. They used to take charge so easily because they were the patterns of behavior we learned when our survival was at stake. Things learned at such times are liable to have a powerful influence on us and are, indeed, not without their utility, but, as Anthony Ryle has said, the aim of psychotherapy is to expand people's ability to live their lives "by choice."

What is important is not to allow these behaviors to control us unconsciously and haunt (shadow) our relationships.

The further along a couple is in dealing with their shadows, the more likely they are to view them and each other with a sense of humor. It was almost a shock to us when we were able to see the comedy of Buck and Nadine instead of acting these characters out with total seriousness. In fact, couples in successful long-term relationships often tease each other about their respective shadows. They are able to laugh and joke about each other's shortcomings in a loving and accepting way. This allows for the other person's growth and transformation. Robert, for example, will often tell people that they should hope they never meet Nadine. When Robert drives the family anywhere Linda tells the children to strap themselves in well, because Buck gets really aggressive behind the wheel. These comments, made in a light and playful manner, make space for the shadow.

Witches and Giants

One reason why fairy tales are so appealing to children is that they can take the unacceptable impulses they feel they have and project them onto the archetypal villains of these stories—the witch and the giant. At other times parents become the objects of these projections.

This might be very well, were it not that when we disown these powerful parts of ourselves in childhood we lose energy and strength in our psyche. We have known many women who stood in sore need of the powerful giant they saw in their male partners in order to deal with their own lives.

Susan, for example, was in the habit of seeking out powerful men whom she then tried to manipulate and live through. She disowned her power, giving it to them, but felt angry and victimized. In therapy, Susan learned to balance her energies and own her power. Rather than going on with a life in which she felt trapped at home, unhappy and passive, Susan decided to return to school, become a professional, and use her powerful intellect to help people in causes in which she believed.

Men, on the other hand, are often quick to cast their female partners as witches and are unable to see how they might have helped create the witchy behavior. Herb, for example, would promise to do something or go somewhere, then break his promise with a casual excuse, or disregard Melanie's feelings to the point where she would be overcome with anger. Blind to her disappointed looks, he was quick to call her "crazy" or "a bitch" when she screamed at him.

In *A Little Book on the Human Shadow*, Robert Bly ironically outlines how these characters from our childhood manage to turn up in our adult relationships and in married life:

> While the bride and groom stand in front of the minister exchanging rings, another important exchange takes place in the basement. During a separate meeting, the mother passes over the son's witch, which she has been carrying, to the bride. An hour after the ceremony the witch is firmly in place inside the bride, though it will take a while for it to show up, because neither the bride, nor the mother, nor the groom knows about this second ceremony.... [A] similar exchange takes place between the groom and the bride's father. Perhaps their spirits meet in the garage—their actual bodies being in church—and the bride's father passes over to the groom as much as he can find of the giant or the tyrant that he has been carrying for his daughter. The bride's father leaves the church door lighter, the groom heavier.

As long as you engage in magical thinking, this "witches and giants exchange" will only keep you trapped in the valley.

Seeing through the Shadow

Ideally, we would be trained as children to look at our faults in an objective manner and to think about them without feeling they were totally unacceptable. Short of this, it is still possible to deal with the shadow as an adult. In fact, as part of an intimate couple, we will usually find plenty of opportunities for getting to know our shadows. With our partners the shadow is exchanged and projected very readily.

If you are starting to dislike an aspect of your partner's behavior, ask yourself: "Is this a part of myself I have disowned?"

How can you come to grips with these impulses in your marriage and use the energy in positive ways? The witch, for instance, can function as a protective force in your life and become a "good witch." The owning of their witch by men would enable them to become better stewards of their relationship's emotional life. Too often, we see men defer to women regarding their mutual emotional well-being. Consequently, they are not aware of the anger that may be building in their partner and don't act to deal with it before damage is done. They spend their time reacting to the anger that their wife expresses for both of them.

Conversely, by owning their giant, women reclaim a lot of the spontaneity and power they have given away to their men. They are then able to stand up to their husbands in an assertive way instead of adopting the nagging, complaining manner husbands find so easy to dismiss.

What characters do you bring to your relationship?

Are you able to own them?

———⟢❦❦⟣———

Exercise

Rate Your Relationship

We play many roles, some real and some mythical, in relating to others. Which of the following roles have you played? Which roles has your partner played?

the critic—the martyr—the witch—the giant—
the baby—the fixer—the magician—the grouch—
the clown—the scapegoat—the messenger—the gambler

• What attributes do you associate with the roles you've played?

• With the roles your partner has played?

• How solid is your relationship?

Answer the following questions honestly:

1. Are you able to communicate honestly with your partner when you are frightened, disappointed, or upset?

2. Are you able to act and speak spontaneously, or do you function on automatic much of the time?

3. Do you feel you are right most of the time, and your partner wrong? Do you try to convince your partner of this?

4. Are you able to share expressions of tender, loving feelings for one another?

5. Do you spend time sharing feelings with one another, laughing and crying and actively listening?

6. Do you avoid certain topics, or are certain subjects off-limits?

7. Would you choose the same partner if you had it to do over again?

8. On a scale of 1–10, with ten being the relationship made in heaven and one being the relationship from hell, how would you rate your relationship?

Down by the salley gardens my love and I did meet;
She passed the salley gardens with little snow-white feet.
She bid me take love easy, as the leaves grow on the tree;
But I, being young and foolish, with her would not agree.

In a field by the river my love and I did stand,
And on my leaning shoulder she laid her snow-white hand.
She bid me take life easy, as the grass grows on the weirs;
But I was young and foolish, and now am full of tears.

William Butler Yeats, *Down by the Salley Gardens*

Chapter Three:

Who Am I Really?

———◆◆◆———

Henry James wrote a short story, "The Beast in the Jungle," about a man who would not commit himself lest he miss an encounter with destiny. Years later, when John Marcher meets May Bartram again, destiny has not yet revealed itself to him. Neither has married; they might yet rekindle their love, they might yet be happy. But Marcher still clings to the belief that something extraordinary will happen to him and he must meet his fate unencumbered. Loving him, saying nothing, Bartram waits with him for the beast in the jungle to spring. It never does. After she dies, while visiting at her grave, Marcher realizes that he is remarkable only for his life's emptiness, its lack of passion.

Fantasies are personal myths. What's usually important is the fantasy. It keeps real people from intruding. They can inspire us or hide the fact that life is unfair, unpredictable, and sometimes frightening. Fantasies can backfire when our partner becomes a "real person" complete with faults. Sooner or later, the true person emerges, which is a good thing because without truth there can be no growth, no change, no transformation.

The process begins when we turn around and face our fears and talk honestly with our partners. We can never tell where these discussions will lead. We have seen couples try to turn toward each other only to find that one or both of them lacked the necessary commitment to the relationship, and to spiritual growth, to make things work long-term. However, it is better to face this sooner than later, and usually such couples prove able to divorce or separate in a loving, accepting way that honors both of them and leaves them in a good place to find another partner with whom to share their lives. On other occasions, we have seen couples who have had terrible experiences in the valley turn toward each other and realize that there was a very strong commitment on the part of both people to making the relationship last.

We believe it is always important for this turning toward each other to occur. Couples in the valley must face the truth and stare down the tigers if they want to create new patterns of behavior and begin to climb the Second Mountain, whether together or in new relationships.

Peter and Dorothy fell in love in the Peace Corps, but when they returned to the United States they drifted apart. In Thailand, the work they did, their common language, the joy of sharing new discoveries, led them to believe they were meant for one another, but Peter wanted to attend graduate school in a big city on the East Coast, while Dorothy wanted to live on a farm on the West Coast and plant vegetables, raise animals, and have children. Peter was eager to get back into the swing of things; Dorothy had learned to appreciate a more relaxed, rural lifestyle. Sadly, fondly, they decided to part.

In their travels, they had accumulated many treasures, furniture and paintings and pottery. Peter took one last look at a batik he had purchased in Jakarta and handed it to Dorothy. "I can't take that," she said. "I know how you love that painting."

"Then you'll think of me when you look at it," he said.

"I'll take it if you take the rug we bought in Nepal."

Peter laughed. "The wool rug with a zillion stitches to the inch. You haggled with the shopkeeper for two hours before he agreed to take what little money you had."

"Not a zillion, silly, but I want you to have it."

And so it went, each giving the other something they prized. And though their lives took different paths, they valued what they'd shared and were reminded of it each time someone admired a mask or asked the origins of an ornately carved box.

Wouldn't the world be a better place if divorcing couples were inspired to affirm and consecrate the joy they'd once shared in one another, rather than tell bitter tales and poison the memory of someone they'd once loved? Hopefully, we will learn lessons that will better prepare us for future relationships.

The other side of the beast-in-the-jungle coin is promiscuity. Chet came to see us because he felt deceived by women and wanted validation for his belief that women were all "manipulative bitches." He said he was interested in commitment, but he didn't want to "work" on a relationship. We discovered that Chet wanted love's rapture without love's responsibilities. Unfortunately, Chet wasn't only fooling himself; he was fooling every woman who believed him to be marriage material. Chet needed to grow up and to recognize that sex and intimacy are not the same thing, but he was unwilling to look at himself, preferring to play the blame game. No doubt he blamed us when we refused to play along.

Regardless of whether a relationship endures or dies, arriving at equanimity is a process, and the couples who make the most progress do so by working on self-acceptance and acceptance of others. What is true is that we need all the parts of ourselves to deal with the challenges of life.

We find that many clients repeatedly "shoot their foot off" because they are unaware of what is unconsciously expressed by their shadows. Trying to get what they want from their partners, they end up with the exact opposite. Their worst fears come to life. Recently, we saw a couple who needed to take back parts of their shadows. Lydia was a svelte, tall, and attractive dental hygienist. She was extremely conservative and believed that women should be subservient to men. As a result, she had a stockpile of hostility in her shadow. Through a plastic smile, she would make disparaging remarks such as, "Well, you know men just don't know how to be considerate," to her husband, and then she would wonder why her husband was so quiet. The more her shadow expressed repressed hostility through such remarks, the more her husband withdrew. Rather than owning her shadow, Lydia would continue attempting to engage him in this manner. They were on a seesaw; the more she said, the more he shut down.

We often see couples on a seesaw, blindly doing more of the same behaviors that never worked. When they can shine a light on their shadows and become aware that these behaviors create the opposite of what they want, change can begin. Unfortunately, in Lydia's case, she was unable to look without judgment and accept her own hostility. Instead, she also projected the hostility onto us and felt that we were blaming her. She left therapy without self-examination, with her shadow stronger than ever. When people are unable to accept their shadows they project those qualities on others. This is very common with people who are often filled with self-hatred. Such people tend to be extremely critical of those closest to them.

In our roles as therapists, we continually alert clients as to how their shadows affect their lives. For instance, there is often a marked disconnect between the adult words coming out of clients' mouths and the childish—and much more powerful—nonverbal communication made by their postures and facial expressions. Examples:

Verbal (Adult)	Non-Verbal (Shadow)
"I'm committed to this relationship"	Looking away (said in a sarcastic, mealy-mouthed voice)
"I really want to be close."	Folded arms, scowl on face
"I need closeness."	Critical look, embarrassed
"I really want to talk to you"	Critical look, embarrassed
"We need to talk."	Looking really limbic (snake-like)

Our clients are usually shocked when we point out the discrepancies between what they say and what they convey non-verbally. Most of the time we don't really see ourselves, so we cannot assess our behavior, but relationships offer us the chance to learn how we come across. With our partner's help, we can hold up a mirror to ourselves and "shine a light within." Then, change and growth are possible. When we can assist clients to look at themselves and their behavior, rather than their partner's, they are surprised by how much they discover the extent to which their unconscious behavior contradicts or frustrates their intentions and needs. Sometimes it feels as if we're wrestling with them for the gun: we point out what they are doing, and if they go back to the same negative behavior we know that the shadow is in charge. The shadow behaviors are deeply ingrained and learned, and it is a difficult process to become free of them.

A colleague once told us that couples often fail to realize that their behavior results in appropriate rewards and consequences. Hannah's behavior was a case in point. At first, she didn't want to move in with her daughter and son-in-law, with whom she'd never gotten along, but when she grew too frail to live alone, she had no choice but to ask Tom and Andrea to provide temporary shelter while her application to the assisted living program was being processed. Weeks turned into months and Hannah continued to live with Tom and Andrea, but now it was her daughter who was unhappy with the situation. Whereas Hannah had gone out of her way to make Tom feel important, she criticized the way her daughter kept house. Tom frequently took Hannah's side, and the subtle, non-verbal cues they exchanged made Andrea bristle. Of course, Tom denied conspiring with Hannah to attack Andrea, and was unconscious of his stance, tone, and manner until we mirrored his behavior patterns. Andrea was more sensitive to her mother's manipulative behavior, having witnessed it throughout her childhood.

If what you convey with your hands, gestures, eyes, and tone of voice contradicts the words you speak, you will not get the kind of response you want. If you want someone to be close to you, but relate to him or her in a harsh voice, using judgmental words and nit-picking behavior, what do you think they'll want to do? On the other hand, if you are kind and loving and fun to be with, people will seek you out.

Ask yourself if you're beckoning to people with one hand while waving them away with the other. Of course, no one is sunny all the time, nor is it the goal of therapy to turn you into "Goody Twoshoes." But the use of self-destructive or negative behavior as a means of getting attention is something else entirely.

Unfortunately, the tendency in our culture is not toward real self-examination. If we discuss problems at all, it is usually with well-meaning friends who see their role as a friend to be supportive to the bitter end. They are unable to believe that the chirpy, friendly person they like to be with is capable of behaving poorly in an intimate relationship. Therefore, it must be the other person's, the partner's, fault. "You must be married to a monster," your friends may say. Friends have not been exposed to the shadow monster that lurks under your skin.

Taking Back Your Shadow

1. We must shine the light within gently and without judgment.
2. Since our shadow contains much repressed material from our childhood, we are likely to feel powerless, vulnerable and immature as we look—but this should not deter us.
3. Since we developed many aspects of this "splinter personality" as a very young child, we may not have words to express all the feelings—pain, grief, etc.—it harbors.
4. Our sense of self is largely established when we are children. Although we have better information as adults, information on its own is unlikely to be able to do away with the feelings of inadequacy and defectiveness that lie in our shadow.
5. It is best to have a "loving witness" to stand by our side as we begin to wrestle with our shadows. Ideally this will be our partner, but at times couples require professional assistance if they are to learn to look without judgment upon their partner's pain.
6. It is impossible to examine our shadows while at the same time engaging in attacking our partners or ourselves. Compassion toward others and ourselves is an essential ingredient in the process of "taking back" our shadows.

In our culture we have tended to use shame instead of healthy guilt in training our children. (Shame is about ourselves; healthy guilt is about actions). As a consequence, it is often difficult to examine the inadequate behaviors of our shadows without thinking that we are inadequate.

The Judge

The majority of our clients who have wrestled with their shadows have found that shadows possess a particularly cruel, faultfinding aspect we call "the Judge." The Judge interferes with getting to know all of your shadow because the Judge's reactions to its contents are so harsh and punitive.

When the Judge is unleashed in a relationship, it usually leads to what we call the faultfinding and blame-gaming that characterize our behavior in the valley. This is the stage in our relationship when it is functioning at its worst.

A client named Wendy wrote in her journal of the torment her Judge caused her by crippling her ability to be natural and spontaneous:

> She is hard—has hard lines; thoughts that pierce you like knives, a hard voice that cuts you…Her lips are so taut you're convinced they will rip if she had to carry on an actual conversation. Nothing, nothing is good enough, perfect enough, worthy enough for her…She feels she holds her ground, gets her worth, by ripping you apart—and she thinks she's doing it for your own good…to spare you the shame of having others discover you're not perfect, or the embarrassment of letting them see you make mistakes…for then they'd see the truth of your unworthiness, the truth of your stupidity. The worst part is she lives through you—so your mistakes are a reflection of her—your sole purpose in life is to make her look good, to please her, to live for her. She holds her breath each time you speak, each time you move, each time you take a risk, will you do her proud?

The target of the Judge can vary from person to person—sometimes the criticisms are directed outward, sometimes at the self. Wendy's judge took Wendy as its primary target and immobilized her as far as relationships went. She couldn't take any risks. She writes:

> Beneath my façade is a very fearful, very insecure, very lonely, very soft woman who longs to be set free. She wants to laugh, or learn to laugh—she longs to find joy in life, as well as bring it to others. She's just never known how to let down her guard.

Wendy needed to restrain the voice of her Judge and learn to be more self-accepting if she was to open up toward life. Unless she could do this she would live in her head, passing judgments upon herself and others. She wouldn't be able to achieve intimacy because her tendency to criticize would push others away.

Unlike Wendy, Ted was an external Judge. An experienced and successful physician, Ted possessed exceptional interpersonal abilities. In his professional life he had been at the center of a highly publicized political conflict, which he had handled with finesse and assertiveness. Yet, he had come to see us about a relationship breakup, which, from his description, clearly had been full of hostility and verbal abuse, though peppered with passionate physical interludes.

Again, as with the two academics, we would have expected Ted to have little difficulty solving his problems. He was more than bright enough to see that his present patterns of behavior were self-destructive, and was capable of learning new ways of communicating with partners. But no matter how "intelligent" an individual is, one should never underestimate the degree to which emotional life can remain under the control of one's childhood.

As is true for most people, Ted's upbringing had elements of blessing and curse. When he was only four years old his father abandoned the family. As a consequence, his mother was forced to devote most of her time and energy to working and to looking after the very young children. Ted, an older child, felt lost and rejected, but responded logically in the circumstances. He learned to deny his need for nurture and affection and to establish a degree of control over his environment by becoming a high achiever. This turned out to be great training for his professional life but was lousy preparation for love and personal relationships. As an adult his emotions were cut off from his highly developed rationality, and what we call his "snake-brain" was in charge of intimacy.

Snake-Brain Logic

The "snake" or "limbic" brain is one of the first parts of our brains to evolve, and we share it with lower forms of life such as frogs, snakes, and sharks. It is concerned with survival in the simplest sense and has very strong survival values. When we are children our survival is dependent on our parents so that disruptions of their relationship are experienced and responded to by our limbic systems. Such responses are powerful and primitive. If parents, for instance, discuss getting a divorce in the hearing range of a young child, the child is likely to respond either by becoming extremely emotional or extremely withdrawn (the "fight or flight" response pattern). Adults can respond along the same lines, experiencing the loss of a relationship as a threat to their very survival as human beings. In this situation, the level of anxiety caused by the idea of separation is so great that it blocks the individual's ability to use his or her neocortex (the part of the brain that carries out higher reasoning).

Because of snake brain logic, people's intelligence may provide little clue as to how they will behave if the going gets tough in their emotional lives.

This was the pattern in Ted's life. Words like "separation," "divorce," or just a sense of his partner moving away from him could lead to his "snake-brain" kicking in, taking over and running his emotional life. Instead of growth, change, and transformation in his relationships, Ted rigidly repeated the same sequence of behaviors:

- Because of a "fight or flight" response at times of emotional crisis, when the relationship ran into difficulties, he either criticized his partner or withdrew from her.
- His fear of rejection led him to keep his partner at a distance. The times when he really wanted closeness only increased this fear and the critical attitude he used to push her away.
- Because he thought of himself as needy and weak emotionally, he was unable to appreciate the impact his critical behavior had on his partner. He was unable to believe that what he said could really hurt anyone.

Like many of our clients, Ted judged himself harshly for his lack of success in establishing a lasting personal relationship, and when a powerful intellect judges a four-year-old's behavior it is brutal. Ted threw around words like "inadequate," "failure" and "stupid," but self-denigration of the type he practiced only fueled the feeling of being small and powerless, which was the root cause of his problems.

In Ted's experience, he was not aware of how his unconscious took charge of relationships and ultimately destroyed them. Like a child, he reenacted scenes from his past, with a deep wish for his partner to change and make everything all right. Rather than shining a light into the darkness of his shadow and learning to face the ghosts of his past, he played the blame game, imagining that his partners "did it to him." He preferred to shine a light on them. Ted's Judge lashed out at his partner. Instead of realizing that he needed to change his attachment style, Ted unconsciously recreated his family drama of criticism and abandonment with a woman he deeply loved. Couples will replay this tragedy at an alarming rate until we all become more conscious in long-term relationships. The unconscious family drama exerts a powerful influence.

He who binds to himself a joy
Does the winged life destroy;
But he who kisses the joy as it flies
Lives in eternity's sun rise.

William Blake, *Eternity*

Chapter Four:

Who Are You?

———◇❤❤◇———

It is said that ignorance is bliss and, for a while, bliss can transport you to places of unimagined loveliness, but, as with shelving dishes, reality soon intrudes. As cited earlier, it could be as simple a defining moment as failing to replace the cap on a toothpaste tube, or as complicated as relating to a lover's children from a previous marriage, but without a grounding in self-awareness, coming to terms with someone else can be frightening and difficult. One must by any means protect oneself. At first, unconscious lovers close their eyes and hope it will all go away. When this doesn't work, the paper bag is donned once again. The world is monochromatic once more, but the pain is diffused along with the light. These people will love again. And again. And again.

A man who had been divorced three times—each time after finding his wife in the arms of another man—came to see us. "What's wrong with women these days?" he demanded. "Why are they all sluts?"

"Where did you meet them?" we asked.

"In a bar next to the adult bookstore," he said. "It's a great place to meet women." He had his eyes "wide shut."

We once counseled a highly competitive couple more interested in being right than being together. We sensed that Sheila had dragged Stewart into therapy in order to punish him, not to salvage their marriage. She reported, "Stewart doesn't want to be here. He's not interested in changing; he'd sacrifice his family if his boss asked him to."

Stewart hung his head in order to glance at his watch, and said, "I'm a workaholic, it's true, but I'm doing it for Sheila and the kids. They spend money like it's water, and the kids are out of control."

"If we had a loving husband and father, we wouldn't need material possessions."

"If I had a wife who knew how to maintain discipline…"

And on it went, each, when it suited them, using the children as weapons in a lose-lose war, then blaming one another when the children acted out. Stewart retaliated by burying himself in work, where he was successful and appreciated. Sheila, we later discovered, had affairs. Through it all, the children suffered and exacted whatever revenge they could.

Some marriages are dying, but where children are involved every effort should be made and every avenue explored before throwing in the towel. Stewart and Sheila were leading double lives to compensate for "not being good enough" at home. They took their pleasure where they could and fought when they were together. For their relationship to have a chance, this had to stop.

Months later, after Sheila agreed to end her affair and Stewart agreed to spend more time at home, we asked them to model certain behaviors for their children, and spend several months defining and reinforcing rules, responsibilities, and boundaries, with attendant consequences and privileges, that both parents and offspring considered reasonable and appropriate. We got everyone to agree it was desirable to live in a harmonious and loving family and that, in order to create that harmony, everyone had to participate. To prevent discord, responsibilities were to be discharged quickly and with good humor. Disagreements were to be aired at certain times and according to specific rules. We facilitated some intense but perforce courteous discussions, allowing everyone to be heard and their feelings validated. This resulted in personal empowerment and a strong sense of belonging to a special family unit. For example, it was decided that everyone should receive a stipend for purchasing clothes and personal items, and that everyone had to live within a pre-set budget. Family outings were also scheduled at these meetings, and special treats awarded to family members who best exemplified a loving family spirit. Their competitive nature was thereby used to enhance rather than erode family values.

We did not suggest that this couple tolerate destructive behaviors but rather that they learn to manage them. Unfortunately, if one partner grows towards transformation and the other partner remains stuck in the valley of shame-blaming, the marriage may no longer be viable. A healthy individual in a couple functions like a healthy cell in the body. The cell has a membrane that is permeable in order to let in the nourishment it needs, and it also has a pump to expel destructive matter. Couples tend to find a partner who has a similar level of functioning. They tend to have a similar tolerance for destructive interactions. If one partner develops healthier boundaries that will not allow destructive behaviors to enter, the relationship will no longer function as it did. In the example above, both partners begin to function like a healthy cell. They both committed to co-creating a healthy family.

Negative Perceptions

To break the cycle of self-destructive behavior we must first understand the power of our past to shape our perceptions of the present. One can think of it like a cell membrane, blocking out some things and letting in others. Many times in our work with couples we are amazed at how their past experiences color their perceptions of the present.

In the following example, a young woman named Kathy was unable to let in the nourishment of her husband's love. She was convinced that her husband, Art, no longer cared for her. As she told us this, Art's face was luminous with compassion. The truth was, Art cared deeply for Kathy, and was on the point of tears. Yet, when we asked her to look at him and tell us what she saw, Kathy could only say "anger." When she continued to talk about feeling abandoned and unloved, Art said quite clearly, "But I *do* love you."

We stopped Kathy again and asked, "Did you hear what he just said?"
"What?" was her reply.

She had completely filtered out his care for her. She had grown literally impermeable to his expressions of love. Further work with the couple revealed that Kathy's father was emotionally immature, alcoholic, and unloving. She saw her husband as the same.

Research into couples in distress has found that when one of them is interviewed and the other watches, the watcher is more likely to rate a comment negatively than would a neutral observer. By contrast, happily married spouses rate their partner's responses more positively than does a neutral observer. Healthy couples are able to screen out negative responses while being more open to nourishment from their partners.

Projection

—◆◆◆—

Projection makes perception.
The world you see is what you gave it,
nothing more than that.
But though it is no more than that,
it is no less.
Therefore, to you it is important.
It is the witness to your state of mind,
the outside picture of an inward condition.
As a man thinketh, so does he perceive.

Foundation for Inner Peace—*A Course in Miracles*

Perceptual Barriers

Some of the perceptual barriers that account for the negative view we may take of our partner:

1. We behave in such a way as to unconsciously set up our partner to act like one of our parents.
2. We recreate our family dramas.
3. Because of our attachment style, we are attracted to those who fit our patterns.
4. Because of family loyalty, we unconsciously commit ourselves to creating the attachments we learned in our family, even though these attachments may be very destructive.
5. We replay the same unresolved conflicts, from our childhood, hoping they will be healed this time by our partners.
6. We relive traumatic situations from our childhood if our partner exhibits a similar behavior that reminds us of those situations.
7. We lose touch with the present reality, and replay old feelings like a broken record.

These are only a few examples of perceptual barriers. Our unconscious sifts reality in distorted ways that are important to identify.

If, when we first fall in love, we worship in our partners the ideals we have projected onto them, in time we may discover they do not live up to our projections. The rapture phase of love usually only lasts between six months and a year. After that we start to notice the more human aspects of our partners. This is threatening, and our response to it can be to go on the attack and begin the process of faultfinding and blame-gaming that pulls us down into the valley. It's a defensive reaction we have observed in hundreds of couples. The problem is that if they are bright and articulate they will be likely to have a powerful arsenal of verbal and nonverbal weapons with which to attack each other. Underneath, as in *The Wizard of Oz*, there is a small man pushing the buttons to make the powerful display—a sad and frightened little man.

But this doesn't mean that faultfinding and blame-gaming can't do any damage. On the contrary, they can inflict much damage at a high rate of speed.

An ancient myth tells of a very young man who finds a perfectly beautiful and valuable pearl in a cave. He aches to own this pearl, but is terrified to discover that it belongs to a huge dragon, so he runs away. He returns to his village and faces life's difficulties. He grows older and "wises up." In the course of life's struggles he matures, and then returns to the cave to see if the pearl is still there. It is! This time, however, the dragon is very small and he can easily pluck away the pearl. What's the lesson here? Wise Up and Shrink Your Dragon!

Similarly, your goal in personal relationships should be to "wise up," shrink your dragon to a manageable size, and win the treasure of mature love that waits for you atop the Second Mountain.

Faultfinding and Blame-Gaming

Unfortunately, in our experience, many relationships never make it past the indifferent valley, the fearsome jungle, or the barren desert. Couples remain in the lowlands, locked in a battle of blame-gaming that does great harm to them and their partnership. Even when divorce or separation doesn't follow, a relationship will often survive by partners withdrawing from each other and living together in a politely superficial way, or continuing to blame-game and verbally attack each other for decades.

We saw a couple who behaved in this fashion for fifty years. They argued with each other over everything:

> *Joe*: I told you to turn left.
> *Martha*: You know I can't hear.
> *Joe*: You've never had any sense of direction.
> *Martha*: You're always so insensitive…

Couples who argue like this can often be in essential agreement over values. Their problem is that they are not good at collaborating, and so tend toward a debating, adversarial form of interaction.

> *He*: The children need to go to bed—it's their bedtime.
> *She*: But they haven't finished their homework.

When these interactions become personal it is serious: the relationship is moving down a rung on the relational ladder from faultfinding to blame-gaming. The partners start to attack each other and put each other down. There is no place for this kind of behavior in a healthy relationship.

> *He*: You're a pawn in the children's hands! You have no idea what it means to be a parent!
> *She*: You're so rigid and controlling! Just like your father!

Before moving on from this form of interaction, we should first acknowledge that our Judge's critical voice often has useful information for us if we can filter out the harshness of its judgments and focus on the behavior it criticizes. We told Wendy, for instance, that if she could translate her self-criticisms into specific ideas for behaving differently and trying to do new things, she would be on the way to combining her high standards with some risk-taking and the achievement of growth.

Many clients have what we call "train wrecks" when they have reciprocal issues that collide with each other. Anthony, a very creative entrepreneur in his mid-fifties, laughingly told us that he and his wife needed a way "to stop the train before the crash occurred." He said, "I think we need a ripcord. It is certainly true that once the train wreck happens we have some debris and damage that needs to be cleaned up."

In Anthony's case, he and Joan have been married for twenty years. They first came to see us seven years ago when their marriage was in deep trouble. They were separated and she had had an affair. They were having train wrecks on a daily basis. Now we only see them every couple of years when they have an occasional "crash." Their train wrecks are usually about the same things; only the situations are different.

Anthony's core issues had to do with being discounted by his family. He was the youngest of three sons and always felt unwanted and devalued in comparison to his two highly achieving older brothers. His wife, Joan, had grown up with an extremely critical mother who made her feel as if she could never win no matter how hard she tried. Consequently, Joan would give up on pleasing Anthony and stonewall him. This made his train pull out of the station, because it felt like the kind of rejection he had felt in his family. They picked up steam as the situation developed, she becoming increasingly critical and he more and more withdrawn.

When we saw them this time, after all these years, we didn't need to get the details about what they were arguing about, because we knew it didn't matter. We had heard many details and many right-wrong games played out between the two. As we were writing this story, it occurred to us that we never did get the specific details, and we think this is significant because it really didn't matter. Details often just get in the way.

When they first came in, they wanted to start in on a victim contest. We reminded them where they were, and they both began to laugh, knowing that an argument was not going to work. They had become experts at looking at themselves and began to laugh at their victim presentations. We then focused on the train wreck, and they were able to reconnect by taking responsibility for their own behaviors. They then negotiated what each wanted and how each could help the other so that both would get what they wanted.

Joan and Anthony have become capable of turning their setbacks into new learning. The first time they called us with a train wreck after "successfully" completing therapy, they felt terrible because they expected that they would never have problems again. Joan left a phone message saying, "The good ship *Lollipop* has sunk." They have since learned that life isn't all or nothing and that love is buoyant.

At painful times, we all go deeper into our souls' wounds and gain a deeper understanding of our partners and ourselves. It seems that we almost need these episodes to "blow out our jets" about issues that trouble us. They enable us to do some emotional housekeeping. Our soul has deep, meaningful agendas related to love and connection with others. The filters that our ego developed in childhood may need to get blasted open so the soul can shine through.

Soft Eyes

In addition to offering the Judge in us a battleground, our intimate relationship can offer us the chance to examine the shadow that haunts our lives. If the relationship can serve as a mirror for us, we can begin to gently shine a light on our shadow. This requires a safe, non-judgmental space, kindness, and what Stephen and Ondrea Levine call "soft eyes."

The eyes of the Judge are fixed and unyielding, while "soft eyes" look with loving-kindness and compassion. Through them we can assist each other in beginning to move away from the past that immobilizes us with fear. Emerson thought of it as taking a plunge:

> Be not the slave of your past—plunge into the sublime seas, dive deep and swim far, so you shall come back with self-respect, with new power, with an advanced experience, that shall explain and overlook the old.

It is not necessary to like the characteristics of our own or our partner's shadow to do this. (We may very well not.) This is because the point of coming to know the shadow is to become free from its control and better able to make choices about how we behave.

Connecting the Dots—Sorting Reality

Try to imagine your partner as an unfinished image made up of 500 dots. As the relationship develops you have connected five, then ten, then fifteen dots, and so on. You've been aware that you haven't really known the other person, and you carry this knowledge with you so that you don't project various qualities and characteristics onto them. You know that you don't completely know them, so you want to see them in as many different situations as possible. By "connecting the dots" of your partner, you create a psychological map of them that allows you to understand and confront conflict together.

It can take years of living with someone before you have connected enough dots to have even an outline of who they really are and what makes them that way. For years in our own marriage, Linda felt criticized when Robert pointed out dangers that she had not considered. For example, he might say: "Have you thought about what could happen if you don't keep your tires inflated?" Of course she hadn't. Robert felt that Linda did not really listen to him about such things because she reacted defensively to his suggestions. She had a childhood issue about feeling misunderstood.

We both felt hurt and misunderstood but finally realized that we simply think differently. Robert's mind operates as if he's playing chess. He's always thinking several moves ahead. Linda's thinking is focused on getting everything it can from the present moment. Neither way of thinking is right or wrong, nor were they things that we were "doing" to each other. It's just that we sort reality in different ways. Both types of thinking have their virtues—sometimes planning for the future is necessary, at other times here-and-now thinking is more appropriate.

The more we have come to understand and accept one another, the more able we are to work as a team, drawing on our shared resources. Now we usually have available to us the style of thinking that fits the situation. Furthermore, we have influenced each other. Linda now keeps her tires well inflated, and Robert gets more enjoyment out of life!

Once this kind of shared growth starts to occur, a relationship has made it out of The Valley and has begun the ascent of the Second Mountain. The couple has begun to reconcile and ahead, atop the Second Mountain, further shared growth awaits them.

Empathy—Reaching Out

Removing the obstacles to a free and full expression of our potential as human beings is extremely hard work—a journey that is never finished. It is a process to be shared in a relationship through empathy. Empathy is the ability to put ourselves in someone else's moccasins—to "feel into" their experience rather than criticize. We ask couples to express empathy for each other by using "soft eyes" and completing the thought "If I were in your shoes, I would feel…." Often, to begin with, they don't fully succeed, expressing their own perspective instead of their partner's. For example, we asked a woman to empathize with her husband regarding his feelings of depression and meaninglessness in his life. She responded, "I think he feels bored with me." This was simply transferring her feelings to him, not trying to understand what he was going through.

If only one partner is willing to work, it may do some good in breaking down destructive patterns of behavior within the relationship, but the likely result is that the working partner's growth will make him or her intolerant of the other's maladaptive behaviors. As previously noted, relationships are usually founded on a similar level of functioning, and if one partner becomes appreciably more healthy than the other, the balance will be upset and the relationship will founder.

When we read fairy tales to our five-year-old granddaughter, Merritt, we make a habit of changing the ending. Instead of saying that the couple married "and lived happily ever after" we say, "and they worked hard to keep a good and happy relationship."

The sad fact is that most marriages fail to maintain a living connection with the transcendent experiences of the phase of rapture. Our culture may be partly to blame: its obsession with self-fulfillment doesn't encourage us to understand the feelings of another person apart from their effects on us. Indeed it can lead us to see our partner's behavior as always "about" us ("it's all about me"), so that if they are unhappy or angry, we immediately feel criticized. Then we fight back or withdraw instead of reaching out.

Having seen the valley, you now have a better understanding of what it takes to nurture a long-lasting, committed relationship. Learning how to face your tigers in the valley early on will help your relationship grow. It is through this understanding that you will not be so fast to panic when trouble strikes.

How to Build a Better Relationship:

Scientific and Spiritual Maps

A couple of years ago we heard about the important work of researcher Dr. John Gottman, who observed thousands of couples in his lab in Seattle, Washington. It was validating to see that his work identified the same important behaviors we had observed, separating couples who did well in therapy from those who decided to end their marriages. We noted several behaviors characteristic of couples in distress. Dr. Gottman calls these behaviors "The Four Horsemen of the Apocalypse": criticism, contempt, defensiveness, and stonewalling. We also observed that whatever efforts one partner might make to get out of this pattern, the other partner was likely to foil. We began to refer to this phenomenon as "shooting your foot off."

On the other hand, Gottman found that there were seven characteristics of happily married couples. We have learned these behaviors the hard way, through our own personal experiences and previous relationships. In more than twenty-five years of observing couples in therapy, we have noted the presence of the following behaviors. We'll discuss them at length below, but in summary, you will know your marriage is improving when you:

1. enhance your love maps
2. nurture your fondness and admiration
3. turn toward each other instead of away
4. let your partner influence you
5. solve your solvable problems
6. overcome gridlock
7. create shared meaning.

From our studies of Jungian psychology and our belief in a universal set of truths, we were not surprised to learn that these behaviors were the same truths described in spiritual wisdom. We are not theologians; however, we have long had an interest in reading the work of great thinkers in the area of spirituality. Recently we attended a lecture by Dr. Francis Vanderwall, a scholar, on the parables of Jesus. The parallels between the principles in this parable about relationships and those in John Gottman's latest book, *The Seven Principles for Making Marriage Work*, are striking.

Since our counseling is based upon a practical spirituality, we have been interested in current research that records in a scientific way what we have known intuitively. The discussion that follows provides a bridge between the valley and transformation. Carl Jung wrote about the self with a small "s" and the Self with a capital "S." The small *self* refers to our individual ego and life drama. The capital *Self* refers to our connection with a spiritual reality much greater than ourselves. It is helpful when we tell a couple that what they are going through is experienced by others. It is comforting to think in "S" questions and to look at our reality in a larger context. The poet Rainer Maria Rilke remarked, "We need to learn to love the questions and to live our way to the answers."

Henri Nouwen's book begins with a description of the parable of "The Prodigal Son," which he called "The Story of Two Sons and Their Father." This material provides a clear and beautiful example of asking the "S" questions. It also illustrates Jung's concept of universal wisdom. Many other examples can be found in spiritual tradition. The parable of the Prodigal Son beautifully describes the ability of our soul to turn lead (our mistakes) into gold (transformation).

There was a man who had two sons. The younger one said to his father, "Father, let me have the share of the estate that will come to me." So the father divided the property between them. A few days later, the younger son got together everything he had and left for a distant country where he squandered his money on a life of debauchery.

When he had spent it all, that country experienced a severe famine, and now he began to feel the pinch, so he hired himself out to one of the local inhabitants who put him on his farm to feed the pigs. And he would willingly have filled himself with the husks the pigs were eating but no one would let him have them. Then he came to his senses and said, "How many of my father's hired men have all the food they want and more, and here am I dying of hunger! I will leave this place and go to my father and say: "Father, I have sinned against heaven and against you; I no longer deserve to be called your son; treat me as one of your hired men..." So he left the place and went back to his father.

When he was still a long way off, his father saw him and was moved with pity. He ran to the boy, clasped him in his arms and kissed him. Then his son said, "Father I have sinned against heaven and against you. I no longer deserve to be called your son." But the father said to his servants, "Quick! Bring out the best robe and put it on him; put a ring on his finger and sandals on his feet. Bring the calf we have been fattening, and kill it; we will celebrate by having a feast, because this son of mine was dead and has come back to life; he was lost and is found." And they began to celebrate.

Now the elder son was out in the field, and on his way back, as he drew near the house, he could hear music and dancing. Calling one of the servants he asked what it was all about. The servant told him, "Your brother has come, and your father has killed the calf we had been fattening because he has got him back safe and sound." He was angry then and refused to go in, and his father came out and began to urge him to come in; but he retorted to his father, "All these years I have slaved for you and never once disobeyed any orders of yours, yet you have never offered me so much as a kid for me to celebrate with my friends. But, for this son of yours, when he comes back after swallowing up your property—he and his loose women—you kill the calf we had been fattening."

The father said, "My son, you are with me always, and all I have is yours. But it was only right we should celebrate and rejoice, because your brother here was dead and has come to life; he was lost and is found."

Let's compare Gottman's principles for successful marriage with the compelling parable of "The Prodigal Son." For a more in-depth theological discussion, we recommend Nouwen's book; what we shall examine here are the embedded psychological precepts that validate the theories Carl Jung postulated in *Dreams, Memories and Reflections* and in other works, namely that if you remove the obstacles that prevent you from accessing your authentic Self, it will lead you toward a transformed life of the "Truths." In order to demonstrate this, here is a brief comparison between Gottman's work and "The Prodigal Son":

John Gottman and the Parable of "The Prodigal Son"

Principle 1: Enhance Your Love Maps

John Gottman found that successful couples have a map of their partner's psychological reality, and understand their partner's interior world. Put poetically:

> *How many loved your moments of glad grace,*
> *And loved your beauty with love false or true,*
> *But one man loved the pilgrim soul in you,*
> *And loved the sorrows of your changing face;*

> William Butler Yeats—from "When You Are Old"

In "The Prodigal Son," the father understands his son's pilgrim soul. Even though the son went away and went wild in the valley of the shadows, the father understood his true repentance and was anxious to take him in again.

In unsuccessful couples we see rigidity in a tendency to hang on to past hurts. They do not have a psychological map of one another's complexity, nor are they able to talk about and explore their "pilgrim souls" together.

It is significant in "The Prodigal Son," that the father didn't need to hear all his son's explanations, why he had done what he did and how badly he felt. The father already understood this. He had a deep psychological map to his son.

Developing a love map for yourself and your partner is important if you wish to understand your inner self and that of the significant person in your life. It is very difficult to explain who we are if we don't know who we are.

Principal 2: Fondness and Admiration

In successful couples we observe a playful fondness and mutual respect. In "The Prodigal Son" the father's unconditional love and fondness for both of his sons is evident. He in fact loves them just the way they are.

Principal 3: Turn Toward Each Other Instead of Away

Gottman has found that when times are difficult, healthy couples have an ability to turn toward each other and dialogue with their conflict. In

"The Prodigal Son," it is significant that the father runs out to meet his returning youngest son. According to Jewish law at the time, a father should never run to meet anyone. The father was less concerned with the rigid laws than he was with the joyful reunion with his son. It was the love that was most important and led to a powerful reconciliation.

Principal 4: Let Your Partner Influence You

In his research with abusive couples, Gottman found that abusers are almost totally incapable of allowing the other's influence. In viewing tapes of couples unable to accept one another's influence, it is not unusual to see an abusive partner discount almost everything that the other says. For example, if one partner says, "The sky is blue," the other may respond, "No it's not; it's blue and red." It's more important to be right than to have love or peace of mind.

In the parable of "The Prodigal Son," the father allows himself to be influenced to give his sons their inheritance early. Again, this went against Jewish laws of the time, because fathers did not give an inheritance to a younger son, nor did they give it early. Scott Peck described this kind of love when he said that true love is "to will the good of the other." It is also important that the prodigal son had to repent to his father. In good relationships, people take responsibility for their own behavior. They do not sit and sulk like a child and wait for someone to come to them. We are shown in "The Prodigal Son" that the oldest son is not yet ready to come to the father. He is caught up in self-righteous thinking. We find this with dysfunctional couples; each feels right and believes the other one should come beg for forgiveness.

Bill demanded perfection and guilt-tripped his wife Sally when she failed to meet his exacting standards. Sally would run away when she felt overwhelmed by Bill's criticism. He blamed her for "refusing to work on the relationship" even when we pointed out that he had missed many more sessions than had his wife. The stress was palpable, and we suggested they take a break from one another. They were able to benefit from separate vacations, and when we next saw them Bill admitted he was too demanding. Sally agreed to discuss issues if the discussions were civil and if Bill would refrain from personal attacks.

Among the ground rules we established were:

- Avoid absolutes like "never" and "always."
- Take turns communicating feelings.
- Moderate your voice and be respectful.
- Listen without interrupting, then verify what you think you heard.
- Acknowledge your partner's feelings and any truth in his or her observations.
- Discuss one subject at a time, and ask permission to change the subject.
- Limit discussions to one hour at most, then schedule follow-up discussions at a mutually agreeable time and place.

Bill and Sally have a long way to go, but they're still talking and trying to understand one another's perspective.

Even when you're in the right, it's unlikely your partner will say, "I see that you've been right all along, and I've been a jerk. Can you ever forgive me? From now on, I'll do it your way." Face it—that's not going to happen. Be gracious enough to accept your partner's acquiescence without insisting on an abject apology.

Principal 5: Solve Your Solvable Problems

Successful couples can discuss conflicts and accept one another's influence, so they are able to solve most problems together. Sometimes they have to accept that certain problems are not solvable, and that they can go on loving each other, respecting their differences while retaining their closeness and joy in one another. In "The Prodigal Son," there is initially an unsolvable problem with the youngest son, so he goes away to learn his lesson. There is also an unsolvable problem with the oldest son, who feels resentful because he has done his duty and is not being rewarded. The difference is that the youngest son learns his lesson, then returns to the father and accepts responsibility for his mistakes. The oldest son pulls away, and the parable ends with his unwillingness to see either his brother's or his father's point of view. It is very significant that the oldest son asks his father why he is having a party for "this son of yours." The father corrects him, referring to "your brother." By so doing, he tries to lead the son toward compassion, toward understanding his brother's point of view. At the end of the parable, the oldest brother is not yet able to do this. He is convinced he is right, and is unwilling to consider another point of view. Self-righteousness prevents many couples from reconciling their differences and creating a joyful existence together.

Principle 6: Overcome Gridlock

In order to overcome gridlock, Gottman teaches that couples must learn to support one another's dreams. To do so, we must first understand our dreams and be able to talk about them with each other. The demise of many a marriage has resulted from the inability of one partner to communicate his or her deep dream and the other partner's inability to understand and support it.

Marge has been offered a promotion, but it means she'll have to travel, and Fred is afraid she'll find someone else. He secretly hopes she won't get the promotion and in subtle ways undermines her self-confidence. His dream is starting a family, but he cannot admit he'd like a baby for fear of appearing unmanly. Fred wants Marge to read his mind and adopt his dream. Insensitive to one another's dreams, they nevertheless create obstacles to their fulfillment. Sometimes, love means letting go; sometimes it means talking, listening, understanding, compromising, and finding a win-win solution to each impasse.

In the parable, the father is able to support his youngest son's dream even though it has immediate tragic consequences. He is able to let his son go to follow his dream. Because it is unselfish, letting go can be the purest form of love. When love returns, as when the prodigal returns, love attains the Second Mountain.

Principle 7: Create Shared Meaning

Happy couples are happy. This may sound obvious, but most people miss the point. In our practice, we have counseled many people who thought of home as a place of strife and who could not imagine what it would be like to be happy at home. Many think they have to go on vacation each year to have shared rituals or joyful times. Their marriages are in survival mode. How sad this is. Healthy couples have many rituals.

On our honeymoon we met a couple celebrating their tenth anniversary. They told us that every month they had a mini-anniversary and would give each other some small gift, such as cigarette lighter or a handkerchief. We thought this a wonderful idea and adopted it, giving each other a little card on the tenth of each month.

"The Prodigal Son" teaches us that God has laid out a banquet for us and, to participate in it, we need to relate to each other with love. Unfortunately, the oldest son chooses self-righteousness over joyful celebration. He thinks of attack instead of love.

As Henri Nouwen puts it: "The world in which I have grown up is a world so filled with grades, scores, and statistics that, consciously or unconsciously, I always try to take my measure against all the others. Much sadness and gladness in my life flows directly from my comparing, and most, if not all this comparing is a useless and terrible waste of time and energy."

People who are hopelessly locked in comparisons and power struggles fail to see that there is an abundance of love and joy for celebrating life on a daily basis. They are their own worst enemies, clinging to the jungle lest their partners find a way out.

"The Prodigal Son" gives us a map to leave our childhood programming and learn to love in mature ways. It is striking that this ancient wisdom is now being documented through the careful and systematic observations of Dr. Gottman.

In reviewing Dr. Gottman's seven variables present in couples in long-term happy marriages, it is sometimes helpful to remember the beginning stages of a relationship, when these behaviors were perhaps commonly expressed:

- *Love maps* refer to a deep understanding of your partner's psychological world.
- *Fondness* can be demonstrated through affection, admiration, or praise.
- *Toward versus away* means that successful couples build up an emotional positive bank account, when they have difficulties they turn toward each other to work them out. Also, on a day-to-day basis they have many varied mindful moments where they are connected, sharing jokes, touching each other's arm, and fixing meals together, for example.
- *Let Your Partner Influence You* refers to respecting your partner's opinions and values. Couples are able to maintain an ongoing friendship through mutual respect.
- *Solve Your Solvable Problems* refers to the ability of successful

couples to learn from experience and benefit from past mistakes.
- *Overcome Gridlock*—Differences are settled through the ability to dialogue with conflict.
- *Create Shared Memories* refers to the rituals, symbols, family pictures, and occasions that reflect the couple's positive bond and shared history.

Valley Survival Kit: Exercises for Facing Your Tigers

In the following exercises, take the time to face your tigers and grow wiser. Each lesson learned can shorten your next trek through the valley. The experiences can be difficult, but there's no better way to learn how to build a strong relationship and ascend the Second Mountain of Transformation. There is hope. So, take a deep breath and follow us...

Ground rules for couple exercises:
- Take responsibility for your own behavior.
- Look at "shadow" material in a nonjudgmental manner.
- Use caring voice and "soft eyes" as you discuss the exercises.
- Remember you are discussing "patterns" or "traits." Discuss these as if they are separate from your self. For example, our pattern of starting a fight when we feel misunderstood can begin suddenly when a trigger event happens, and it can continue for days. How can we manage this tiger?
- Develop specific strategies to manage the tigers. For example, one couple developed the following strategies:

When I feel misunderstood, I will:

Stop action
Go be by myself
Blow off steam with exercise
Focus on what I am reliving
Refrain from attack thoughts about my partner
Ask myself if I choose "attack thoughts" or "peace of mind"
Write in my journal
Go back and dialogue the conflict with my partner when I am calmer

Exercise 1:

Review these variables and discuss specific ways that you might include or develop these behaviors in your own relationship.

Dr. John Gottman identified four behaviors that are very detrimental to a successful marriage:

Criticism: This is criticism of the person and not some specific behavior.

Contempt: Nonverbal negative expressions such as frowning, rolling eyes, or verbally expressing contempt.

Defensiveness: Instead of being able to discuss the problem, they read criticism into everything that's said.

Stonewalling: Nothing gets through, nothing is heard, so change is impossible.

Exercise 2:

How might you defeat these negative behaviors?

In order to counteract some of these behaviors, practice:

- Appreciation: Express appreciation on a daily basis.
- Validation: Support one another for speaking positively, particularly in front of children or other family members.
- Stopping actions: Develop signals to stop a negative escalation. Some of the couples we worked with have used different signals. For example, one couple would say, "Let's have a cup of tea," to indicate that they needed to calm down. Another couple would say, "We know where this ends."

Exercise 3:

How could you regularly express these positive behaviors?

Exercise 4:

Relationship Questionnaire

Separately, you and your partner complete the following with brief, clear answers that summarize your feelings:

1. What I most want to change about the relationship is...
2. What I like most about the relationship is...
3. What I wish my partner understood about me is...
4. What I wish I understood about my partner is...
5. Briefly describe your "dream" (ideal) relationship.

Exercise 5:

What I Want in a Relationship

List ten things you want in a relationship. Then discuss them with your partner. For example:

- "I want to be able to differ in opinions, even disagree, without creating estrangement or feeling estranged myself."

- "I want to hug several times a day."

- "I want to be able to change, and feel safe."

Exercise 6:

How to Know When Your "Snake Brain" is In Charge

When your "snake brain" is in charge you exhibit self-destructive behaviors, though, based on your fears, they make sense at the time. Here are some examples of frequent "shoot your foot off" behavior by a middle-aged professional man we recently counseled:

* The "snake brain" (limbic) was in charge of intimacy despite his superior intellect.
* His emotional reasoning was cut off from his higher reasoning when in an intimate relationship.
* He was unable to see his impact on his partner because he felt small and powerless.
* He was more afraid of rejection than he was of the consequences of his self-destructive patterns.
* He unconsciously pushed his partner away by being critical because of his fear that she would push him away.
* He repeatedly "shot his foot off" by pushing her away when he really wanted closeness.
* His primary repertoire of responses was attack or withdrawal, fight or flight.
* He rigidly repeated the same behaviors though they never worked.

Identify and discuss the kinds of "shoot your foot off," self-destructive interactions that you engage in.

Discuss behaviors you might use to calm down before you resume an argument. For example, one client goes out and waters the flowers to calm down but laughs, "He better not come near the hose!"

Exercise 7:

Keep a Journal

Keeping a journal is an excellent tool for learning about yourself and your relationship. The following format is simple and allows you to observe your behavior over time and to set goals. You and your partner should keep separate journals. You may keep your journal private or share entries with your partner.

Purchase a book with at least 365 pages, lined or unlined. Make a brief entry for each day of the year, leaving space for five years on the same page. Include:
* A summary of what was most important for you that day.
* Any questions or lessons you found meaningful.
* An affirmation for the same day the next year. (Affirmations are the goals, stated in present tense, which you hope to accomplish in the future.)

It's O.K. to miss a day because you'll still have enough entries for comparison over five years.

Example

April 22, 1999
Divorce is final today; very sad but determined not to repeat same mistakes.
Read *Why Marriages Succeed or Fail*, by Dr. John Gottman.

"No matter how tough, no matter what kind of outside pressure, no matter how many bad breaks along the way, I must keep my sights on the final goal." (*Billie Jean King*)
Affirmation: I am capable of a loving, long-term relationship.

April 22, 2000
Dating a new woman named Mary—plan to take it slow—get to know her background, family and philosophy.
Affirmation: I am centered, happy and whole.

April 22, 2001
Broke up amicably with Mary—learned to be good adult partner, enjoyed her company but feelings are not strong enough for marriage. Read "Balancing Heaven and Earth," by Robert Johnson. He used symbol of cross for balance within ourselves— horizontal side = feet on the ground; vertical bar is spiritual, transformation.
Affirmation: I now have a relationship that includes friendship and passion.

April 22, 2002
Very painful breakup with Lucy after only three months. Still in love, although I know she is not right for me (drugs, unable to commit). Nevertheless, I miss the intense feelings.
Affirmation: I now balance my thinking and feelings in my ideal relationship.

April 22, 2003
I think Jane is right for me—exciting, but stable—we are friends and lovers. Plan to go for some counseling to discuss our lifestyle differences and consider marriage.
Affirmation: I now have my ideal marriage.

Shall I compare thee to a summer's day?
Thou art more lovely and more temperate:
Rough winds do shake the darling buds of May,
And summer's lease hath all too short a date:
Sometime too hot the eye of heaven shines,
And often is his gold complexion dimm'd;
And every fair from fair sometime declines,
By chance, or nature's changing course, untrimm'd;
But thy eternal summer shall not fade,
Nor lose possession of that fair thou owest;
Nor shall death brag thou wander'st in his shade,
When in eternal lines to time thou growest;
So long as men can breathe, or eyes can see,
So long lives this, and this gives life to thee.

William Shakespeare, *Sonnet XVIII*

Chapter Five:

Who Are We?

———◦❦❦◦———

Among couples, few members are willing to take responsibility for their behavior. It's almost always the partner's fault. Andrea and Skip were no exception to this general rule. Married for close to ten years, they were on the verge of divorce when they came to see us.

"All Skip does is criticize me," Andrea complained. "He says it's for my own good, but I feel like a prisoner in my own house. I wish he weren't so critical. He makes me feel bad about myself and then complains when I'm not all perky and vivacious. Skip thinks he's my friend but he acts like my enemy. He doesn't have friends because he never has anything nice to say about anyone. I wish he were more tolerant, but he's attached to his prejudices."

Not surprisingly, Skip blamed Andrea for "letting herself go to seed. She's not the same girl I fell in love with in high school," he said. "I feel cheated." He gave her a dirty look and added, "And I'm not prejudiced; I'm discriminating. There's a difference, you know."

It's been said that women marry men in order to change them, while men marry women believing they'll never change, and this was certainly true in Skip and Andrea's marriage. They both needed to make some changes, but they weren't able to until they stopped blaming each other and took a long, hard look at themselves.

The Path to Mature Love

To experience the transformation to lasting, mature love we must learn that the joys of our first, innocent love will be imperiled by experience. This is entirely normal, in fact unavoidable. If we use those experiences, we will develop greater depth of character; we will transform our relationship and climb to a higher plane. Without the pain that comes with experience, we do not mature, we do not grow stronger and more capable of genuine commitment. It is important that couples who share pain do not dismiss it. Shared pain, which Scott Peck refers to as "creative suffering," enables relationships to evolve. Some couples even say that only those whose hearts have been broken can truly love.

Many of the people who come to see us are locked into what we call "all or nothing" thinking. They believe that if their relationship is not perfectly happy, one or the other of them must be "sick." Holding to this attitude makes creating a healing environment in therapy more difficult. Couples who are working on their relationships have to feel safe to reveal their whole person. If they feel that aspects of their identity are going to be labeled as "sick," they will be understandably reticent.

"There's such a thing as too much equality," Mark complained the first time we saw him. His wife, Phyllis, was forever meting out chores and making sure no remark went unchallenged. There needs to be room for people to be themselves rather than symbols of political correctness. On the other hand, people stuck in unequal relationships are usually unhappy, and unhappy people make for unhappy relationships.

As a child, Phyllis felt neglected. Her parents were divorced and her mother worked long hours to provide for her and her two younger sisters. Phyllis was baby sitter and maid from the time she entered kindergarten until the time she graduated from high school and her sisters were old enough to take care of themselves. She was grimly intent on making sure no one would ever again take advantage of her.

Phyllis brought to mind the joke about how many feminists it takes to screw in a light bulb (answer: "That's not funny!"), but she herself hadn't much of a sense of humor. We couldn't help laughing when she excused her puritanical views by pointing out that she was the adult child of an alcoholic. Whether it's an excuse, a politically correct rationale, or a dodge, there has been entirely too much focus on victimhood lately. Warranted attention is brought to how children can be victimized in families, but things are taken too far when victimization is accepted as a way of being and relating. One celebrated victim sued San Francisco claiming that riding on a cable car had turned her into a nymphomaniac.

People who think they are innocent victims believe it is their partners who need to change; they themselves are perfect. This attitude is reinforced when seeking advice from friends when a relationship is going badly. Your friends are partisan and no doubt quick to assure you that it's all your partner's fault. However, if you think you are an innocent victim, you won't be motivated to change and grow. Victims believe that all that needs to happen is that their partner have a personality transplant.

"Your mother doesn't drink," Mark said, "and neither do you."

"No, but my father did. That's why Mother left him."

"But you were four years old when they were divorced," Mark said.

"Well, I must have been affected by it," Phyllis said. "Every time I hear a beer commercial, I want to sing along."

Certainly the relationship you are in can, indeed, hamper your development. You can stop, and be stopped from, graduating out of experience to transformation. None of us are cupcakes. We must take responsibility for our own experiences and face the fears they expose.

The Enemy Within

Bill was raised in a family where he was smothered and rigidly controlled by his mother. He manages a corporate business, while his wife Pat stays home and manages the household. She is pregnant with her first child. Both are in their mid-thirties.

Because he felt smothered by his mother, Bill insists on going out every night and drinking with his pals. He probably has an alcohol problem but will not admit to it. He feels Pat is trying to control him because she wants him to stay at home. When she confronts him about going out, Bill says, "There you go again."

Pat, on the other hand, is afraid of being abandoned. Thirty-four and pregnant, she feels vulnerable and unprotected. One of the younger children in a very large family, she too felt neglected as a child. Each time Bill goes out, it triggers her anxiety. Bill isn't involved with another woman, but he's still irresponsible about the relationship and about Pat's feelings.

Whenever she calls him on it, he accuses her of trying to control him. In fact, it's the other way around. By his actions, Bill controls Pat.

For this situation to improve, Bill and Pat need to face their own tigers. Pat's fear of abandonment fuels her anxiety when Bill goes out at night. She must learn to identify the source of her anxiety and come face to face with it and the feelings it creates. For his part, Bill needs to confront the tigers of control looming from his past before he can share those feelings with Pat. Once Bill and Pat begin sharing their feelings, a new, clearer line of communication can open and a deeper relationship can occur.

Avoiding tigers is tantamount to repeating your failures. People who avoid facing their tigers tend to repeat history. If they divorce, they re-marry believing that this time they have found a partner with whom the fairy tale will happen, and they will "live happily ever after." If they hang on to the relationship as it is, then they do so out of fear and self-doubt. Neither of these alternatives brings with it true love or security. In fact, they obstruct our growing stronger and climbing out of the valley toward authenticity and deeply meaningful relationships.

At some point we all stumble on the journey toward acceptance, love, and transformation on the Second Mountain, but if both partners have the commitment, they can use their conflicts as growth experiences that help them make the climb together. Sometimes one partner will be ahead, sometimes the other; both can reach back and give a hand up to the partner who is trailing behind. And all the time the pair will be developing relational skills such that, should they fall all the way back into the valley, they can get out again much more quickly. Ultimately, couples will even learn to enjoy the process of enduring the valleys and exulting on the mountaintops together.

We find that couples who decide to climb the Second Mountain to-gether slip on occasion, but face the new challenges that come their way with minimal recourse to the faultfinding and blame-gaming that char-acterize our behavior. This is where having the right *gear* counts. We'll talk about this more at the end of the chapter.

Differentiation

In *Passionate Marriage*, David Schnarch describes the concept called *differentiation*. This is the ability to stay close to someone and maintain your individuality at the same time. It is probably the most difficult task we have to learn in our adult life because it requires us to have a firm identity and be able to passionately relate to another at the same time. We often find that couples are capable of one or the other. As Schnarch puts it, a differentiated person in a couple is able to say, "This is what I want. How can I help you get what you want?"

In our experience most people can only respond to the first statement or second question. We see many who are clear about what they want, but who cannot compassionately help their partner. On the other hand, we are reminded of the woman, discussed earlier, who realized in a session that in ten years of marriage she had never once asked for what she wanted. She was shocked to realize that when they made the decision to marry, all she thought about was whether he wanted to marry her, never even asking herself whether she really wanted to marry him.

We are born alone and die alone. In between, if we are lucky and skillful, we love and are loved. Taken together, they constitute our life. We must be able to live life fully and, at the same time, help those we love do the same.

Gail was sure Harry loved her because he was so jealous. He had to know everything she did when they weren't together. It made her feel wanted, protected, and secure. After marriage, however, Harry's jealousy and possessiveness made no sense to Gail. "I wanted to join the church choir, but he thought I was attracted to the choir director. He wouldn't even teach me how to drive, so I was stuck inside until he got home."

After Gail discovered Harry was having an affair, she sought help from us. We suggested Harry join her in counseling, but when she invited him he grew nasty, even struck her. Gail might well be better off without Harry, but she's now pregnant and afraid to tell him because he might beat her.

The first thing Gail must do is discover herself. She must learn to see herself as separate from Harry. After she figures out who she is and what she wants, she would be able to notify the police if Harry hit or threatened her. She could learn to be more closely in touch with her instinct for self-protection. At present, she's incapable of doing so. She maintains that Harry loves her, when it seems to us that Harry loves only himself.

Learning New Behaviors

When people see us to work on their relationships, they often ask, "Can people really change?"

We believe that change is based on awareness, so we tell couples how to increase their awareness of each other by the technique we call "Connecting the Dots," which was explained in Chapter Four. We share with them our experiences as a marriage and family therapist and a psychiatrist, which have convinced us that people can, indeed, change dramatically in the way they relate to one another. By having faced our own tigers we are able to reassure others that they can, too.

One couple we saw were a dominant husband named Bob, and his submissive wife, Cathy. Although an imbalance exists in many successful relationships, over the years of interacting in this way, Cathy had built up resentment that was poisoning their relationship. Finally, they decided to separate. However, Bob loved Cathy and their children very much and wanted to save the marriage if he could. He came into our office determined to change the way he behaved.

During the next six months, Bob radically altered his way of interacting with his wife. He became much more sensitive toward her and supportive of her needs. He was able to look at the effects of his domineering behavior on the family as a whole and realize that he did not want the consequences. At the same time, Cathy learned to be more assertive and to speak up for her needs in a constructive way. She stopped relating to him through fear and began to relate with sensitivity and compassion.

When couples are able to detach from their patterns of behavior, recognize what is destructive and hurtful, and ask, "What can we do about this?" a wonderful beginning for change opens up. Such couples can learn to observe their behaviors and the inevitable consequences, and ask questions about what they can do differently.

Then, the question for couples in difficult relationships is not "Can people change?" but "Are we willing to give up our investment in old behaviors and learn new ones?"

It is your investment in old behaviors that tends to make you dismiss your partner's reacting negatively to something you do. Your attitude may be "It's not my problem; get used to it." But if something is a problem for your partner, it's a problem for you. And if the problem is to be resolved, each partner must be willing to hear the other's pain, and not dismiss it.

To reiterate, both as individuals and couples, we must accept that the joys of our first, innocent love will be imperiled by painful experience—and we must use those experiences to transform our relationships and climb to a higher plane. Without the pain that comes with experience we do not mature; we do not grow. It is important that couples who share hurts do not dismiss them. Shared pain enables relationships to evolve.

Once we have learned to shine a light on our shadows and faced our tigers in the valley, we can begin to climb again toward the Second Mountain of transformation. Were transformation easy to achieve, the divorce rate would not be so high. It requires practice, self-examination, and the reflection learned in the valley in order to reach transformation. The higher we climb, the fewer the setbacks, and the faster that couples are able to rebound.

Climbing Toward Transformation

Joseph Campbell defined marriage as "the recognition of spiritual identity." In *The Power of Myth*, he says, "Marriage is not simply one's own thing…it is in a sense doing one's own thing, but the one isn't just you, it's the two together as one. Simply because people have been to a ceremony and obtained a marriage license does not mean that they are capable of sustaining this kind of transcendent union."

We chose the metaphor of two mountains to chart the course of love because the kind of combined consciousness, unconditional love, and acceptance that Joseph Campbell describes cannot be easily reached. It is a goal, a summit, that we strive to reach and from which we often fall before facing our tigers, accepting ourselves, and becoming mature, compassionate, loving partners. On the journey toward a transcendent union, we have to face our fears and projections and put aside our simplistic belief in rapture that continues "happily ever after." But, as we climb love's second mountain, our load will be lighter because of the time we spent in the valley working through issues. Every time we have to return to the valley, we can emerge lighter still, better able to continue the climb. That's why it's important to look upon every failed relationship as a learning experience, and why it's usually not a good idea to jump from one relationship to another without pausing to learn what we can from the relationship that ended.

Richard was thinking about placing a personal ad when he came to see us. He'd started writing it a dozen times, but wasn't sure what to say. Should he emphasize his best traits, he asked us, focus on what he's looking for in a mate, or be humble, hoping to score points for honesty? The more he thought about who might respond, where to meet, and what to say, the more frightened and confused he felt. "Should I forget about meeting someone this way? Am I better off going on blind dates that my friends arrange?"

When he'd gotten his hopes for a future relationship off his chest, we asked him why his last relationship had failed. "Thelma just up and left me," he said. "I don't know why. Women are always dumping me for no reason at all."

When we suggested that introspection would serve him better than dating at this juncture, he reluctantly agreed to complete some exercises (see Valley section) that would help him understand his behavior patterns. Until he knew himself, how could he know what to seek in a partner?

In order to begin the process of transformation a couple needs to have four conditions for change:

1. Both partners value and wish to continue the relationship.
2. Each partner is willing to hear the other's pain and recognize how he or she is contributing to it.
3. Each partner is willing to change his or her behavior where necessary.
4. There is no physical violence in the relationship, no substance abuse, and neither partner engages in hidden activities.

Delia came to see us because she wanted new furniture, but Buster, her husband, refused to buy anything for the house. An aging hippie, the son of socialist parents, Buster said that he'd be happy with milk crates for furniture, if only their children were admitted to Harvard. They have launched their children, but their clothes come from Goodwill. "It's not fair," Delia cried. "Life's not fair," Buster replied. "Look at the Dodgers' payroll; they should be in first place." Communication wasn't a problem when everything was "groovy" during the '60s, when they met as flower children. How could they start to talk to one another about their issues?

First, they had to stop blaming one another for their situation. Then, we helped them see how their past dominated their present. Their parents had lived through the Depression, and as young adults they lived on very little. Times had changed, but they hadn't changed with the times. We encouraged them to hear one another's pain and to effect the changes they could make. (Winning the pennant for the Dodgers was not within their purview.)

If both people in a relationship are presenting themselves as adults when the child inside is really in charge, problems tend to escalate.

Mike and Sue described to us a traumatic episode, which occurred during the afternoon and evening of one day in their relationship. In the afternoon, they talked on the phone, and Sue let Mike know how much pressure she felt at work and how she needed his support. The conversation was a good one, and she looked forward to its continuing when they were at home together that night. Unfortunately, several horrendous incidents at Mike's job intervened, so that by the time he came home he was in a very different state of mind: distraught, depressed, and wanting to be alone. Sue had prepared a gourmet dinner for the two of them, but had not otherwise expressed to him any of her ideas about what the evening was going to be like. She was devastated by how withdrawn he was as he attempted to process what had happened to him since her call.

Finding Mike distant and distracted, Sue interpreted this personally, taking it as a rejection. Rather than deal with this, she began to pick on small things, and became critical. She told him off for leaving the paper lying about the house and for leaving tools out in the garage. She was dismissive about his wanting to watch the football game on TV and about how he had handled an incident with the children. Finding the criticism intolerable, Mike decided to get out of the house by lying about having to go back to the office. At that point, she launched a full-blown verbal attack about how he was never there when she needed him. This was "all or nothing" thinking; only that afternoon she had found him helpful and supportive.

The "tigers" at play here were that Sue had a developmentally disabled sister who demanded most of her parents' time and attention. Sue had felt valued only when she was able to help her parents deal with the pressure. She felt her parents weren't there when she needed them. Mike, on the other hand, had had a mother for whom nothing was ever good enough. She was highly controlling and criticism was her principal weapon.

Mike and Sue had created what we call a mutual "creature feature," with tigers from the past taking the leading roles. She felt devalued, unloved, starved for attention, and worthless. He felt controlled and criticized, as if he could not win. Both were reliving their childhood.

When they came in for their session, we concentrated on these childhood issues. When we got down to that level, Sue began to cry a great deal and talk about the past, when she had felt she only achieved recognition in her family through performance. Mike talked about the effect it had on him to feel that someone else was trying to control him, and how he had felt that the only way to protect himself was to leave.

It was a very touching session, because the two really had a great deal of love for one another. We talked about the importance of dealing with the times when the child was in charge, and being able to articulate that in such a way that they could get the things they each wanted from the relationship—understanding and a feeling of connectedness.

This couple has learned to shine a light on their shadows and to face their tigers in the valley. Now they are climbing again toward the Second Mountain of transformation. It took practice, self-examination, and reflection in the valley in order to reach transformation. Even though they might visit the valley again, it is not as frightening with new skills and knowledge. They will rebound faster, grow stronger as a couple, and become more intimate. There is exhilaration from going higher.

We are always touched when we witness such love, closeness, and combined consciousness. This level of intimacy cannot be sustained all the time, but it is a goal, a summit that we should strive to reach. On the journey we must face our fears and projections and put aside simplistic "they lived happily ever after" views of how a relationship works. As we climb the mountain our load will be lighter because of our time in the valley. We encourage couples who are having problems to work diligently together to learn the lessons that they need to learn in the valley. Even if they decide to divorce, they will have a much better idea of what went wrong and how to climb toward transformation in the future. In fact, it raises red flags when we hear a client blame a previous partner for the demise of a marriage, because they have not faced their tigers. They are likely to repeat the same cycle and wind up stuck in the valley with a future partner.

Transformation is characterized by taking responsibility for the life that we create. The term "New Marriage" in no way suggests that people should dispose of current partners or troubled relationships and start over with someone new. On the contrary, the term is used to remind us of today's new relationship dynamic and how couples might redefine and renew their relationships to make them stronger. A "New Marriage" can refer to newlyweds who are just beginning their journey, to remarriages of those stalled in the valley, or to long-term couples.

By the time we reach Transformation Mountain, a number of developmental hurdles have been faced. We have enjoyed the bliss of first love and endured the fear and heartbreak in the valley of experience.

Michelle and Richard managed to transform themselves from angry, fused identities to shared, separate completeness by undertaking serious individual and joint self-analysis. At the point when they came to see us, the only vision each had of their marriage was of the other's faults. Michelle had a tendency to feel abandoned, Richard a tendency to anger and aggression. When a problem arose, Richard would withdraw, fearing he might say or do the wrong thing; Michelle, feeling abandoned, would jab, poke, or insult in order to get some reaction. Richard would explode, break things, and bite himself. Finally he bit Michelle. Sensibly, they decided it was time to separate for a while. Doing this enabled them to start working on knowing themselves as individuals without the other's influence. They learned that they had become fused and had become unable to think of themselves individually. (The reverse of this was a tremendous closeness that played a part in sustaining them through the bad times.)

Through group therapy and regression hypnosis, Richard explored his urge to bite—he found out about a very scared two-to-three-year-old child who was never sure what trouble he would get into at home if he spoke, and who feared his father's, mother's and older brother's tempers. (Another brother later confirmed for Richard that their home had, indeed, been a scary place to grow up in. This was important for Richard.) He also renewed his spiritual life through prayer and, after a long search for a model for overcoming intense anger, found one close to home: his father, who had become more approachable after he quit the police force and started teaching. Richard developed a resolve not to take his anger out on anyone or anything.

The couple continued to have contact: Richard would invite Michelle over to his place for dinner and Michelle would feel romanced and special.

Richard would share what he was learning about himself and Michelle learned to listen without interrupting and telling him that what he was doing or saying was wrong. Both of them started to miss not being together at special times like holidays.

After six months of therapeutic separation and individual work, Richard moved back in with Michelle. Now both appeared to have a firmer sense of their own identities, though their intention was to continue working on themselves and not to try to "fix" each other. Richard had developed a capacity to verbalize his feelings, which made it easier for Michelle not to feel ignored or abandoned. If he got angry, he could remove himself without cost, because he would first explain to Michelle what he was going to do, and why. They also discovered what a marvelous tool laughter could be for defusing tension: sometimes in the middle of an argument one of them would have trouble pronouncing a word, or knock something over accidentally, and they would dissolve in giggles. The issue would be defused, left behind. They called it the "Team Giggle." This proved a positive way for them to defuse potentially harmful interactions.

Three years after undergoing self-analysis, they described themselves as "stronger, happier…two separate, complete people who enjoy sharing our lives together." Since Richard's depression badly affected his work, this has included "sharing the process of rebuilding income together and supporting each other." They are a team.

It is very important to become conscious of how you transmit your desire to connect with another person. You need to communicate that you want to connect with him or her, and monitor your tonal quality for sharp notes. Check to see you are not giving mixed messages nonverbally, but that your nonverbal cues also show an interest in connecting.

This takes a great deal of practice, though it may seem simple enough on the surface. One of the most difficult things that we have to learn in our adult life is to remain close and separate at the same time. We are unable to maintain a clear sense of our intentions without a clear sense of self. It is also necessary to learn compassion for the other person in order to communicate consciously. Carl Jung used the term "individuation" to define the process of a person becoming separate, an indivisible unity or whole. To complete this process, we must learn to "own" our shadow, recognize projections, and embrace our uniqueness. Jung felt that it was important to note that the individuation process is not limited to our ego or self-centeredness. "Individuation does not shut one out from the world, bur gathers the world to one self."

In her lovely book, *The Cloister Walk*, Kathleen Norris mentions that we have a tendency to turn our grief into grievances. If we do this, we will not go deeply enough inside our own conflicts but rather stay on the surface, blame-gaming. Norris points out that the answer to the question in Psalm 34 ("which of you desires life and covets many days to enjoy good?") is "keep your tongue from evil, your lips from speaking deceit, depart from evil and do good, speak peace and pursue it." She adds that when the "thorns of contention" arise in daily life, we should daily forgive and be willing to accept forgiveness. We are not capable of such forgiveness without learning the individuation that allows our hearts to become spacious enough to contain our intentions while maintaining compassion for the other. The Bible instructs us, "love one another as thyself." In our experience, we find that people are either too focused on self-love or on the needs of the other.

Heroic Moments

Peggy Papp, a well-known marriage and family therapist, suggests that it requires "heroic moments" to break out of self-destructive patterns. It requires courage and determination to put aside the "cookie cutter" we use to slice life up in the same old and familiar ways, and begin the process of change.

It is helpful to refrain from self-criticism as change is in process. Change takes time and is complicated by the dynamics that exist between two people. One partner can confuse the other's self-image.

The dictionary tells us that a camera lens "controls the rendering" of color and that the definition of "to render" is to "cause to be or become." How your partner sees you—renders you—can cause you to become something you are not. In the course of our practice, we have often been amazed by the ability of partners to unconsciously do this to each other.

Here's an example:

Jackie and Mark were able to move from reliving the past to embracing the present. It started some years ago when Jackie came for help because she was depressed and unhappy. She had been the youngest child in a happy family and described herself as very independent. She had traveled extensively, had many friends, and remained close to her family.

The trouble began when she became involved with Mark, who had a domineering mother.

At first Mark reported that he was attracted to Jackie because she was totally different from his mother, and indeed she was. However, as they gradually grew closer, he asked her to stop traveling and stay by his side. She was in love and wanted to be with him, so she complied. However, once they were together, he started to work late. She complained. He worked even later and then began to drink with friends after work, never asking her along. She complained even more.

The incident that brought Jackie in was a blowup after Mark had stayed out until three in the morning without calling her. She reported that she lost control and called him "immature, inconsiderate, and selfish." Guess what he called her? A "dominating mother." In a matter of months he had rendered a woman originally attractive to him because of her dissimilarity to his mother into a carbon copy of her.

Nevertheless, by working with Mark, we found he was able to back up, look at the overall pattern, and see the destructiveness of his approach to interpersonal difficulties. In the end his behavior was truly "heroic." When he became aware that Jackie had significant problems from her childhood, he didn't use it as a cue for faultfinding. He encouraged her to seek professional help and redefined their relationship as a friendship, despite the fact that he really felt much more for her than she did for him.

Later they were able to discuss this inequality of passion and, though it was extremely painful for him, he was able to face the fact and examine the way it appeared to repeat a childhood pattern where the love he felt for his parents was not reciprocated. He was able to let go emotionally and bring the relationship to a conclusion without rancor. He was even able to support Jackie as she became involved with another man, and later he became involved with someone else too.

In describing this process Mark said, "Though the [first] relationship did not develop into the picture of what I had wanted, the dissolution had not torn me to pieces. I found those parts missing since boyhood and became a complete man. I understood the source of my pain and was full of forgiveness. The fire, which could have burned, had instead forged my soul into strength. The effort was intense and the healing quite thorough. I had grown into a good partner and could now find one. The attraction would not be between two wounded selves. From a healthy center, I saw a woman with equal maturity and was able to attract my present partner, who now gives me appreciation, encouragement, support, respect, and understanding. Our focus is on continued growth…"

The Power of Combined Consciousness

Alone we can do anything, but together our minds fuse into something whose power is far beyond the power of its separate parts.

Accept this Gift: Solutions from a Course in Miracles
As members of an intimate couple we need to be aware of the energy that is created between our partner and ourselves. We call this energy *combined consciousness*. It is greater than the sum of its parts. The combined consciousness is a third member of any committed relationship. This is how a committed relationship really looks:

In *Embracing the Beloved*, Stephen and Ondrea Levine refer to this energy as the "Beloved, the energetic suchness to which so much devotional literature, poetry, and scripture refer when attempting to express the personal experiences of the sacred."

The Levines write about how they use the energy of their combined consciousness for the development of their relationship. In a spiritual here-and-now process, they view one another as "beingness constantly unfolding" instead of as "static stereotype[s]" based on "cultural or gender differences." The Levines argue that when members of a couple have a difference with their partner, they often attribute it to gender, making statements that begin with, "All women…" or "All men…" Statements of this sort may be used to justify a lifetime filled with judgments and hatred, instead of love and acceptance. Looked at this way, seeing ourselves as separate dilutes combined consciousness.

Let's look at this more closely. In the early days of Christianity, the emphasis on love and forgiveness created a union of souls among Christians by means of which a sense of sin was shared, not individualized. It wasn't until the fifth century and the influence of St. Augustine that there was a shift in emphasis toward the kind of individual confession we know today. Once we saw ourselves as separate and individualized, instead of as a part of God's plan for all humanity, the way was opened up for some people to also think of themselves as "special."

Attacks on others were then justified by focusing on points of difference, like skin color, creed, or country of origin. Today that focus even includes the part of town people live in, or the clothes they wear. This habit of thought has seeped into the conduct of our most intimate relationships, so that nowadays people often use gender difference as a justification for either attacking or dismissing their partners. Some even go so far as promoting the idea that male and female humans come from different hemispheres or planets!

Additionally, the experiencing of shame in isolation has placed stress on the individual psyche. This is what powers faultfinding and blame-gaming; when our sense of shame at the problems we experience in a relationship gets to be too great, we attempt to shift it. We blame our partners.

To avoid blame-gaming, and to put ourselves on the right track for developing a combined consciousness with our partners, the Levines suggest we learn to look at our partners with "soft eyes"—to watch them without judgment, but with compassion and loving-kindness instead.

In her therapeutic practice, Nancy Thomas trains the angry children sent to her by setting limits while establishing contact with "loving eyes." These children, abandoned or abused as infants, had learned to distrust and to "get even" with society for the way they were treated when helpless. Thomas teaches her wards to be "respectful, responsible, and fun to be around" by meting out consequences for inappropriate behavior, but doing it with love and humor. Evidence of humor is in the laughter provoked; evidence of love is in the eyes, "the window of the soul."

In her beautiful novel, *Before Women Had Wings*, Connie May Fowler shows how this can work. She describes the plight of a little girl called Bird, who is physically and verbally abused by her alcoholic parents. She has no safety net of love and acceptance until she meets a wise black woman named Miss Zorah.

Bird's mother is suspicious of Miss Zorah and forbids Bird to talk to her. However, Bird soon recognizes the wisdom and healing balm of Miss Zorah's unconditional love, her acceptance of life and other people, and her devotion to her fellow human beings. Ironically, it is Miss Zorah who convinces Bird's mother to get help by hearing her pain without judging her, by looking at her with "soft eyes." Miss Zorah also teaches Bird to face difficulties and leads her soul to safety. She gives Bird great advice for relationships when she advises her to "pick up your fear and stare it in the face." This is what we mean when we say you must "face your tigers."

Similarly, you need to stare down the fears that alienate you from others and cut you off from the power of combined consciousness. A potential grace lies all around you, if only you can come out from under the shadow of your past and stand in the fullness of its light. Until you do, you will "relive" the past as a prisoner of your childhood instead of living in and embracing the present. Remember that your soul is complex and cannot be boxed into easy, superficial categories. Your soul has a capacity to grow ("beingness constantly unfolding"). We thrive on space and a sense that we are connected to forces greater than ourselves. If we box the soul in, we stunt its growth.

Marion Woodman, a Jungian analyst, shows how love can heal in a relationship when she describes what it was like, after years of marriage, to see her husband for the first time, free of her own projections. She heard him rattling around in the kitchen attempting to poach an egg. At first she thought in terms of her "shoulds" and became judgmental of his inadequacy as a cook. But then she let go and just saw him, a man in Bermuda shorts that showed his spindly legs, offering her an imperfectly poached egg. She felt profound love.

For us, the use of "soft-eyes" in our intimate relationship fits with the Bible's exhortations "to love thy neighbor as thyself." First, we need to use the "soft eyes" of love to look at ourselves. Then, once we have achieved self-love, we must use the "soft eyes" to look at others. Even as he suffered on the cross, Christ was able to look with "soft eyes" upon the men who had put him there and say, "Father forgive them for they know not what they do."

GEAR

In order to pass through the lowlands without being devoured by tigers or snakes, without getting lost, and without sinking into the quicksand of self-pity, we need help finding the skills and equipment required for climbing the Second Mountain. Proper gear will help us overcome the obstacles created when we were children:

GEAR = Growth + Empathy + Acceptance + Responsibility

Part Three

The Second Mountain:
Transformation

To see a world in a grain of sand
And a heaven in a wild flower
Hold infinity in the palm of your hand
And eternity in an hour.

William Blake, *Auguries of Innocence*

Chapter Six:

Communication and Intimacy

G enuine communication can be easy or very hard. Verbal communication involves first recognizing the existence of a thought
or feeling, then finding the words to express that thought or feeling—
and that's just the half of it. What is said must then be heard and interpreted,
and the interpretation verified. Most of the time, we think communication has occurred after our expression is acknowledged, but there's no way
to know unless the meaning is checked. For example, "When you said you
were lonely, did you mean you wanted my company?"

Insecure people tend to communicate in vague terms, hedging their
meaning because they are fearful that what they say will prove unacceptable. However, communication that is clear, direct, and concrete leaves
little room for misinterpretation. Nothing facilitates good communication better than active listening skills.

Active Listening

Active listening can help an insecure partner become less afraid of expressing feelings. It conveys the message that feelings are not bad. When
you demonstrate by active listening that you are neither judging nor con-
demning what your partner says, your partner will be better able to accept
your feelings, no matter what they are.

Active listening promotes feelings of warmth and closeness. The
experience of being heard and understood by another person is in itself

satisfying and usually makes the speaker feel good about the listener. When you listen empathetically and accurately to others, they understand that you are putting yourself in their shoes. And when you get inside another person's shoes, it produces feelings of closeness, caring, and love. Even in the absence of a solution to an expressed problem, active listening facilitates problem solving by engendering warm, close feelings.

Active listening also inspires a speaker to listen to your views with an open mind. It's natural for people to want to listen to what you have to say if you have listened to what they have to say in a nonjudgmental, loving way. Your partner is also more likely to be open and straightforward with you when you engage in active listening. In this way, both partners trust enough to communicate clearly and fully.

Active listening involves feedback, repetition, eye contact, and compassion. The following phrases convey that you care about what your partner is saying: "You seem to be saying…"; "It sounds like you feel…"; "I sense you strongly believe that…"

Communication Tips

When you discuss issues with your partner, be genuine and be present. Don't let your mind wander. Maintain eye contact. If your partner is upset, empathize with how she or he feels. Use "soft eyes" to convey the idea that you're on their side. If either of you tends to change the subject rather than deal with it, create an agenda of issues to discuss as a reminder to stay on task. If you disagree with what your partner is saying, wait your turn. Don't interrupt. When it's your turn, instead of saying, "You're wrong," try, "I see things differently."

If your partner is not forthcoming about an issue, ask what's wrong in a way that doesn't invite a yes or no answer. Ask, for example, "What's troubling you?" rather than, "Is something troubling you?"

When a problem has been identified, don't offer a solution. Ask, "What will you have to do to fix it?" or, "What can you do about it?" or, "What's in store for you?"

If your partner responds, "I don't know," ask, "What information will you require in order to know?" or, "What do you know about it so far?" or, "How can you find out more about it?"

Other helpful questions might be: "How can I help you?" or, "If the same thing happened again, what would you do?" or, "If you had it to do over again, what would you do differently?"

If you disagree with your partner's course of action, don't reject it as "wrong" or "silly" or say something like, "that's just like you." Instead, try, "What if it doesn't work out the way you'd like?" or, "What will you do if it doesn't get you what you want?" or, "Let's brainstorm an alternate plan if this one doesn't work out?" or, "Where do you suppose it will lead?" or, "What are your chances for success?"

We find it helpful for couples to work as a team to solve their problems. Even when they disagree, couples are better able to dialogue with a conflict as friends. It is useful to speak in terms of "we" instead of adversarial wording. For example, John and Sharon, middle-aged professionals, learned to ask "How can we solve this problem?" They described a delightful incident when they were traveling across the country in a van with their in-laws and two teenage children. They began to bicker, and a difficult trip became unbearable. John stopped the van on a deserted road and invited Sharon to step out. He asked, "Are we going to do this for another five hours?" Sharon shrieked, "I certainly hope not." He then suggested that they turn on the radio and sing and resume the argument later. They both felt it was in their best interest to can it, and reported that five hours later they had forgotten what the argument was about.

Communication Techniques

Say it again, Sam. Tell your partner what you heard. For example, "You think I won't like who you really are, is that it?"

Clear the air. Make sure you understand the meaning your partner attaches to certain words. For example, "When you said 'We bumped heads,' did you mean we argued or were stymied?"

Tie it up. You may need to help your partner draw a conclusion. For example, "It sounds like you care about me but are afraid to show it because you think I don't care as much about you."

Check it out. Verify that your assumptions are correct. For example, "Am I right in thinking that's how you feel?"

Plain and simple. Use concrete terms rather than vague concepts. For example, "When you say you feel bad, is it guilt or depression or something else that you're feeling?"

Recapitulate. Before ending a discussion, summarize what your partner has told you. For example, "Let's see if I have this right. You've been withdrawn and angry because you think I'm going to leave you the way your father left your mother when you were six years old."

Silence is golden. It's better to remain silent than to muddy the water by asking too many questions. Allow space for you and your partner to think things over.

Explore alternatives. Instead of offering a solution to a problem, try brainstorming to come up with other possible solutions. Avoid rejecting any off-the-cuff idea—nothing blocks brainstorming like criticism. Laughter dispels tension. Find the humor in the situation, but don't make fun of your partner or belittle your partner's problem.

Don't judge or evaluate your partner's problems. What's trivial to you may not be trivial to others, and vice versa. Don't assume your partner sees things the same way you do. Your beliefs and convictions may be deeply ingrained but they are not universally held.

Listen with your heart as well as your mind. Don't pretend to understand what your partner means. Ask for clarification. For example, "I want to understand how you're feeling and thinking, but I'm not sure I do. Please tell me again, using different words."

Let me not to the marriage of true minds
Admit impediments. Love is not love
Which alters when it alteration finds,
Or bends with the remover to remove:
O no; it is an ever-fixed mark,
That looks on tempests and is never shaken;
It is the star to every wandering bark,
Whose worth's unknown, although his height be taken.
Love's not Time's fool, though rosy lips and cheeks
Within his bending sickle's compass come;
Love alters not with his brief hours and weeks,
But bears it out even to the edge of doom.
If this be error, and upon me prov'd,
I never writ, nor no man ever lov'd.

William Shakespeare, *Sonnet CXVI*

Chapter Seven:

What Really Comes after "Happily Ever After"?

———◦❤❤◦———

Sometimes couples will come into our practices and want us to judge their arguments. We decline. Our job is to help them manage the energy of their combined consciousness toward creative, rather than destructive, ends.

Here are some tips for creating combined consciousness:

- Focus on the process between you instead of on individual differences.
- Work at accepting your partner's imperfections and your own.
- Look for the deeper meaning in your repetitive arguments, e.g., jealousy of your partner's relationships with others may reflect a lack of meaningful connection in your own relationships.
- Become curious about patterns of behavior you may have learned in your family of origin and that you may be repeating with your partner.
- Ask yourself how you can use the energy of your combined consciousness to enhance your life instead of letting it fuel destructive behaviors.
- Ask yourself how you and your partner can make each other's lives larger, not smaller.
- Create together a picture of what your ideal relationship would look like. Refer to it daily.
- Try to resist participating in interactions that are ultimately destructive of your combined potential.

Is it easy? Of course not. Most of our clients have needed encouragement and support in confronting the ghosts of their past. Joe, for example, was a strong, self-confident executive who ran a multimillion-dollar business and who would dissolve in tears when his mother put him through her daily guilt trip. From childhood, Joe had defined himself as "inadequate" because he believed that if he were more clever, charming or whatever, he could make his mother happy and she would give him what he needed emotionally. He learned to be a clever entertainer, which stood him in great stead as a businessman but didn't unlock his mother emotionally, as he'd hoped. As a consequence, no matter how great his success with other people, Joe always felt a secret sense of inadequacy.

Joe laughed when we told him that one day he would feel compassion for his mother, instead of terror. "Yeah, right!" he retorted.

But in the course of several years, after his unexpressed anger had come to the surface and much grieving had taken place, Joe was able to see that his mother's unhappiness was not his "fault," and he was saddened by the way she needed to define herself as a "martyr." Now he views her with compassion and loving detachment. He can even make her laugh, and certainly doesn't allow her to put him through guilt trips anymore. His relationship with his wife has improved as well.

Choosing Your Own Attachment Style

One of the turning points of Joe's therapy occurred when he did an exercise that directed him to give back unhealthy characteristics of his mother's attachment style and reclaim parts of himself from his shadow. Some examples of his insight on this assignment are as follows:

I Give You Back: The Despair and Hopelessness
I Reclaim: My Optimism, Eagerness, and Faith

I Give You Back: The Long Failure of Your Marriage
I Reclaim: The Right to have a Healthy, Strong, Happy Marriage

I Give You Back: The Underhanded Criticism
I Reclaim: My Assertiveness and Being Appreciative

I Give You Back: The Distance, Coldness, Formality
I Reclaim: My Warmth and Closeness, My Ability to Reach Out or Withdraw, To be with Others and to Be Alone

I Give You Back: The Obsession with What Others Think
I Reclaim: My Self-Direction, My Being Centered

I Give You Back: The Belief that You are the Only One Who Knows What is Right
I Reclaim: My Ability to Develop Standards and Values from My Own Life

I Give You Back: The Narrow Sense of Correctness, Perfection, Moral Superiority and Formality
I Reclaim: My Imperfect, Sprawling, Messy, Hairy, Smelly, Changeable Nature

Transformation Exercise

Following the example that Joe used, address the attachment style that you wish to return to a particular family member. It may be a father, mother, sibling, stepparent, or another member of your extended family. Make a separate list for each family member to whom you would like to give back aspects of their personality. You then reclaim the fragmented parts of your self.
It is important to remember that the focus is on your inner healing rather than on holding onto blame of family. The purpose is to become conscious of the attachment style that limits your own fulfillment in relationships.

The Trek to Transformation Mountain

We were delighted to have our perspective on relationships confirmed by the Most Reverend Frank Tracy Griswold III when he said:

> A transformed heart is a heart that has been cracked open by God's love. It is a heart willing to have its tendency towards accusation and judgment overruled by the same voice Jesus heard at his baptism, a voice that speaks to each one of us and says, "you are my daughter, my son, my child, my beloved, my chosen one in whom I delight and in whom I rejoice: with whom I am well pleased simply because you are…"

To climb the mountain a second time, our hearts must be cracked open by God's love. So many of us are so hardheaded, and have learned to be so hardhearted, that we need some pain to crack us open and get us out of our pattern.

For spiritual progress to occur, the heart must be willing to stop making accusations and passing judgments. It must leave behind the faultfinding and blame-gaming that characterizes our behavior in the valley. Valley behavior doesn't permit a true reverence for our partner. Our partner is someone we have chosen, and by choosing him or her we have committed ourselves to their well-being.

Through active listening, compassion, and combined consciousness, you can achieve empathy, know what your partner feels, and desire what your partner wants. When you and your partner do this together, you will have scaled the Second Mountain and attained love's summit. Peacefully confident and powerfully motivated, you will rejoice in your relationship.

You will be delighted by your partner. If you are no longer having good times with your partner, you'll know that something has gone wrong in the relationship. The literature of marriage and family therapy is full of examples that show how healthy couples are light and joyful with each other most of the time. They rejoice in their relationship.

Your partner will be one "with whom you are well pleased simply because you are." Accepting partners for who they really are is one of the most difficult things in a relationship. In the rapture phase of love, we don't see the flaws in our partners; they are ideal. Then, in the valley, we start to see and react to their underbelly. If we wish to climb out of the valley and begin to learn and grow together, we must accept our partner's faults. You can change yourself, but you cannot change your partner; only your partner can do this. In *The Spirituality of Imperfection*, Ernest Kurtz and Kathlyn Ketcham write:

> The literature of pop therapy and pop spirituality seems to make the assumption that along with the divine child within us there is a "divine" way of interacting with each other—a method free of mistakes, flaws and imperfections. Parents can be taught how to raise their children without wounding the holy child within. Adults whose inner child has been wounded can recover their primary essence. But for anyone familiar with a long tradition of spirituality of imperfection this view is inherently flawed.

Transformation Mountain is not a final destination but a continuation of our life's journey. As we climb the mountain, our load has become lighter because of our time in the valley and the GEAR that we have acquired. Couples continue to face challenges and learn to be even better climbers. On Transformation Mountain, it is possible to put our flaws into a better perspective. For example, we were recently inspired by a couple in their forties with two teenage children. Although she has terminal cancer, they function as friends and remain mutually supportive.

The first time Janet walked into our office she exclaimed "Oh gosh, Linda, you are wearing white!" When we looked puzzled, she explained that she could no longer wear white because they marked her body with a red pen for cancer radiation treatment. We were both very touched by her courageous humor and hoped that we could cope nearly as well with cancer. Even though this couple functions at such a high level, there are times when the stress plunges them into the valley. They came to us for assistance in dealing with particularly stressful times. They did not require much help to get them back on track because they were skilled climbers.

At times, couples come to us expecting the magic that they have read about in pop psychology. They believe that if we can identify the essence of how they were wounded, they will be divinely healed. This is a variation on the magical thinking of childhood. For all the grace and beauty on Transformation Mountain there are still challenges—and visits to the valley—along the way.

Dylan Thomas wrote that the purpose of love in this life is to "unbolt the dark." In her book, *Love is Stronger than Death*, Cynthia Bourgeault describes this process:

> "…as I look back on the time with Rafe, I am struck by the fact that in that pure becoming we both so yearn for, it was not the best stuff in us but the worst that God transformed to make the new person. The very force that Rafe most feared in himself, his attraction to me, emerged in the refiner's fire of love as true commitment. And the worst in me, my desperate clinging, gradually melded into something I would never have believed myself capable of—true devotion."

The flame of love purifies the defects from our childhood. Combined consciousness does not take place on the First Mountain of erotic attraction.

"It is not a product of attraction but rather a purification: a commitment with which the partners adopt the spiritual practice of laying down their lives for each other—facing their shadows, relinquishing old patterns and agendas, allowing all self-justification to be seen, brought to the light and released."

On Transformation Mountain, love adds to the evolution of our souls to allow us, individually and as a couple, to live more fully in the light. Love should provide for the deepening of the celebration of life. A spiritual marriage provides a path for our souls' development. Carl Jung referred to the sacred marriage as "*hieros gamos*." A typical example of this union of archetypal figures is the representation of Christ as bridegroom and the Church as bride. Sacred literature from many traditions is filled with examples of the bride and bridegroom. These images represent a powerful force in our consciousness leading toward the bonding with another in order to illuminate the forces that stagnate the growth of our souls.

Love can trap and stagnate us in the valley if we do not have a partner who is willing and able to accompany us to Transformation Mountain. One such example from our practice was an attractive middle-aged couple with three daughters. When we first saw the couple, Larry was just ending his third affair. In fact he had been involved outside the marriage for nearly nine of their fifteen years together. He was emotionally unavailable to his wife and daughters during the majority of the marriage. Although he was willing to remain with his wife, he had no motivation to make any changes. As we saw it, his behavior not only stagnated the growth of his own soul but also the souls of his wife, their three daughters, and the three women with whom he'd had long-term affairs. This situation kept everyone stuck. We know that love is a trap when we are stagnated and unchanging. The poet Rilke wisely observed, "lovers—were not the other present, always spoiling the view! ... Behind the other, as though through oversight, the thing's revealed...but no one gets beyond the other, and so the world returns once more." The "thing" revealed, which is a view of a higher reality, can be blocked by our significant "other." We are only able to live on Transformation Mountain when we have dealt with our childish, egocentric thinking. A couple can keep one another stuck for a lifetime at the level of the valley and only catch occasional glimpses of the heights of Transformation Mountain.

St. Bernard of Clairvaux described erotic love as the original and most authentic expression of who God really is. When we fall in love on the first mountain we get glimpses of this reality. Our descent into the valley allows for a cleansing of our self to create room for a higher conscious-ness. "For certain very high cosmic purposes it is essential that man acquire a soul. The normal way of doing it is through the union of the sexes," according to J. G. Bennett in *Sex*. Other dyadic relationships under the fire of emotional passion may also provide for the soul's evolution. Rela-tionships that are stuck in the valley not only prevent our soul's evolution but maintain the hurts and barriers of childhood.

Climbing Transformation Mountain

PEAKS	STEPS
Insight	Look for love & laughter No longer think as a child Break out of the prison of your own ideas Make better choices if you are not happy
Conscious Attachment Style	Joy amidst suffering Conscious mindfulness of the moment Ideal vision of the relationship Love as much as you can from wherever you are
Integrated Sense of Self	Wholeness Unity with others Spacious self that transcends the ego Able to be active & receptive
Respect for External Forces	Recognition of complexity of world & universe Giving others the benefit of the doubt Acceptance of forces greater than ourselves Motivated by love instead of fear

Steps up Transformation Mountain

Our true identity as spiritual beings
Choose love instead of fear
Serve mankind with our unique gifts
Nourishment of combined consciousness
Possibility Thinking
Think of our pain instead of my pain
Take responsibility for the life you created
Become magician of your own life
Individuation
Active v. passive
Refrain from judgment of self & others
Acceptance of self & others
Ask self, Is this behavior loving?
Cooperation
Compassion for Self & Others
Express gratitude for one another
Refrain from comparison games
Serve as a model
Self confidence

The Transformed Heart

In raising children and in building relationships, it's important to accentuate the positive. To see your partner in a more compassionate light, don't take your partner's positive aspects for granted and don't focus on negative traits. If you slip into "all or nothing" thinking by demanding perfection, you will overlook all the small kindnesses and acts of consideration your partner performs. We are always impressed in therapy by how some couples with the gravest of problems continue to help each other. Focus on what is dear in your partner.

Faith in God, appreciating His love, will help you feel more compassionate toward an errant partner. Live in His love, enter His joy, and abide in His peace. Don't allow yourself to become mired in everyday life.

Your relationship with your partner can help you focus on the higher spiritual reality that sits atop the Second Mountain. Sometimes all we need to pull us out of the valley and begin the climb is to raise our eyes to this higher reality and focus there. Research indicates that couples who share spiritual principles in an active way are happier together. We make a practice of saying a prayer together each evening and expressing a way in which we appreciate one another. We recommend this small ritual to couples. Try it.

In the "Song of Songs" in the Bible, the unnamed lover (believed to be God) watches us from behind the scenery of our everyday world. If we are caught in our own ghostly dramas we do not see the joy, love, and miracles splashed across our lives. Love and acceptance are the lens through which we can see the graceful present.

We urge you to celebrate your relationship. Take time to relive the memories and lessons you have achieved. Rejoice over the happy moments, and be grateful for surviving the tough times in the valley. After a visit to the valley, the horizon of transformation beckons you. Your relationship will be continually evolving through your journey. Give it all you've got!

In *Connecting with All the People in Your Life*, L. Huffines writes:

Compassionate listening has two components: the head and the heart. Both are valuable but either, by itself, is incomplete. 'Head' knowledge alone becomes cold and distancing, compassion alone can turn into empty sentiment.

Unfortunately, many couples polarize, with one partner assuming the voice of reason and the other partner the voice of emotion; together they make one complete person. This pattern is often described by the trite phrase, "communication problems."

Transformation Exercises

—◁♥♥◁—

An active listener:

- fully commits to listening
- clearly intends to understand as deeply as possible the message of the other
- seeks to understand the reality of the other through compassion and empathy
- refrains from verbal and nonverbal judgments
- is physically and mentally ready to listen
- validates the partner's reality before expressing his or her opinions
- balances head with heart
- remains present in the here and now
- is open to new learning about one's own behavior
- self-evaluates and is able to laugh at one's self

Exercise 1

Discuss how you can better develop and utilize active listening skills in your relationship.

Exercise 2

Create a Dream Journal and record your dreams. Discuss with your partner, if your partner is interested and empathetic.

Exercise 3

Reprise.

How committed is your relationship? Now that you've read this book, answer the following questions again:

1. Are you able to communicate honestly with your partner when you are frightened, disappointed, or upset?
2. Are you able to act and speak spontaneously, or do you function on automatic much of the time?
3. Do you feel you are right most of the time, and your partner wrong? Do you try to convince your partner of this?
4. Are you able to share expressions of tender, loving feelings for one another?
5. Do you spend time sharing feelings with one another, laughing and crying and actively listening?
6. Do you avoid certain topics, or are certain subjects off-limits?
7. Would you choose the same partner if you had it to do over again?

Appendix

———◈◈◈———

Recording Your Dreams

In order to use dreams for the benefit of an intimate relationship, the dreams must be recorded; otherwise, most will be forgotten or distorted over time.

There are many formats for recording dreams; the one we use, which you may modify to suit yourself, is based upon the stages of analysis. We divide the page into three columns. In the first, we write down what happened in the dream, without judgment or any attempt at interpretation. At this stage, attempting to "understand" the dream may interfere with its proper recollection. In the second column, we write down any association with the dream's contents (people in the dream, things that happen, where the dream occurs, objects that appear, etc.). We also note any key-word symbols, and follow the associations freely. In the third column, we place ourselves back in the dream and write down the feelings/emotions we experienced at each stage.

Here is an example of a recorded dream:

Dream Date:
Dream Title (written later):

Dream	Associations	Feelings
I was chasing Rick with a baseball bat	Baseball bat- weapon, strong	Anger, rage, strength
	Rick (Tony's best friend): abrasive, loud, insensitive	
I hit Rick several times until he yelled: "Stop! I'll turn the TV off!"	TV—source of contention between Tony and me	Satisfaction

Dating the dream is important: it provides a context for reference. You may find that dreams remain with you for many years.

After completing each column, we review it, ask what insights have been gained from it, and write them down. We also trace our behavior and actions in the dream; for example, are we standing still or are we moving in a particular direction? Are we behaving passively, aggressively, assertively? We give ourselves permission to feel any emotion that might have emerged from the dream. At the same time, we ask ourselves, "Am I confronting what needs to be confronted here? Does the dream show action or inaction creating a better or worse situation for ourselves and others?" Finally, when we feel we understand what the dream has to tell us, we ask, "How would we rather have interacted?" The answer can be used to rewrite the dream, creating a new one in which we interact with the dream images and symbols in a better, more satisfying way. The process helps to create new patterns of interacting in our daily lives.

Except in the presence of a trusted therapist, it is probably best not to reveal your dreams if your partner is not willing to listen to them nonjudgmentally or carries a grudge about your relationship, i.e., if he or she does not have "soft eyes." Revealing your dreams to someone else requires trust, and should only be done with someone who holds you and your dreams as "a sacred trust and a wonderful adventure."

Here are some guidelines for sharing dreams with your partner:

- Write down your dreams and explore them in the manner outlined before sharing them.
- Don't share your dreams without permission. If your partner seems resistant, explore the reasons. If resistance is still there, honor it.

Tell your partner what you want from her or him as a listener. For example: "I want you to listen and then ask questions that will help me explore the dream message further." These may be questions like: "How did you feel when you fell down?"; "Have you ever felt like that in normal life?"; "Does the person who pushed you remind you of someone?"; "How would you change the dream if you could?"; "How would you change your way of interacting in it?" Questions like these are usually more helpful than for your partner to attempt to interpret your dream.

When you share your dream, make sure you have your partner's undivided attention. Ask for what you need. If time is not available immediately, see if you can set up another time during the day.

If sharing your dream with your partner seems unhelpful at any point, explore what the reasons might be. Honesty is paramount, but you will have to be understanding of your partner's lack of expertise. You must also appreciate that issues raised by the dream may be sensitive for both of you. It will be a chance to be caring and compassionate in return.

If your attempt to share your dream fails, there will probably be other people in your life who will be interested in sharing dreams with you.

Dreams are catalytic, stirring personal responses in listeners as well as dreamers. It is only normal that a partner will occasionally want to interpret a dream. When this happens, ask yourself honestly if you want to hear someone else's interpretation. The chances are that it will be different from your own, but it is unrealistic to expect anything else. You might find it helpful to ask your partner what they would be exploring if the dream were theirs.

Ultimately, dreams are a mystery. Since they are featured in the earliest known writings, we know that people were speculating about the origins and meanings of dreams as far back as 2000 BC. But the key to understanding dreams has not yet been found. We do know, however, that dreams are sometimes prophetic. They can tell us about daily events that happen to people we know, as well as earthshaking events that affect everyone. At other times, they communicate, on a literal or symbolic level, messages that help us understand our thoughts, feelings, and interactions more clearly. Sometimes they provide us with affirmations that stay with us for the rest of our lives.

Dreams have been regarded as sacred in almost every religious tradition. As you begin to share your dreams with your partner, you are embarking on a venture into a "sacred realm," a miraculous realm. Think of your dreams in this manner and they will gain in richness and depth. You will feel united with your partner, other people, and all of creation. You will dwell within the mystical way.

The Enneagram—A Window Into The Self

In *The New Marriage*, Doctors Linda and Robert Miles set forth a practical and easy-to-understand approach to building stronger and more authentic relationships. The process must begin with the realization that all humans are complex beings and that the key to growth, both personally and in relationships, is to better understand who we are and who the other is in all our parts. Understanding ourselves and others would be so much easier if Flip Wilson's famous character, Geraldine, was right when she sassily said, "What you see is what you get."

Unfortunately, it's not that simple. In fact, when it comes to understanding both ourselves and others, what you see is almost never what you get. The reality is that life would probably be somewhat mundane and even boring if real personal growth and growth in relationships were that easy. It is not. For we are not simple beings. Not one of us. However, the good news is that the forces that reside within each of us, including the "shadows" and the "tigers," though enormously powerful, can be understood and even embraced as being normal and vital elements of the human experience. But the knowledge of self and others comes only to those who are willing to seek and to accept, even celebrate what they find along the way.

Fortunately, there exist today some extremely significant and helpful resources to get us started on this journey. This is due to the fact that, regardless of the great variety of theories that have been advanced by those during the modern era—from Freud to the present—who have given their lives to the study of the human personality, today there is almost universal agreement that, though each of us is unique, all human beings operate within a limited number of personality patterns. Simply put, by using well-established personality inventories, we can discover much more about who we are and how we operate (and who others are) than we ever could have imagined before doing so.

The most researched and still the most utilized of these is the Myers-Briggs Type Indicator (MBTI). During the mid-1950s, a layperson, Isabel Myers, and her mother, Kathryn Briggs, expanding on Carl Jung's Psychological Types, devised a questionnaire for identifying personality types. It was designed to identify the sixteen patterns of action and attitude that, in their view, encompass the full range of human personalities. This inventory was so well received that in the 1990s over a million individuals a year were taking it. Today, thousands of therapists find that utilizing the MBTI provides them invaluable insights into the workings of their clients, and provides an extremely useful frame of reference within which to conduct the therapist-client dialogue.

Though many management consults also find the MBTI to be a helpful tool for fostering better communication and problem solving within the work environment, other inventories seem to me to be more useful and adaptable for this particular use. The Performax Personal Profile is both robust and particularly useful in this arena and is our personal favorite. The point here is that both inventories, and no doubt others, provide rich and valuable information as to who we are and how we are most apt to interact with others.

However, for those who want to begin the journey into self-discovery and want to utilize a tool that is as powerful and rich as either of the above and, in our view, surpasses both in the amount of available and accurate information concerning not only one's basic personality type and style, we strongly recommend the Enneagram.

We must confess that when, several years ago, a friend suggested that we get acquainted with the Enneagram, we looked at each other and thought in unison, "not another inventory." The word itself, *Enneagram*, had a somewhat strange sound to it. We quickly found that it was anything but strange. The reality is that the Enneagram tradition goes back hundreds of years, having been an ancient and remarkably accurate description of human personality in all its diversity. The word itself is taken from the ancient Greek *enneas* (nine) and *gramma* (something written), and is visually depicted by the nine-pointed star. Use and study of the Enneagram was shrouded in secrecy as it was passed from culture to culture, continent to continent, until well into the twentieth century. But it was the work of professional clinicians over the past twenty-five years that has brought the Enneagram into recognition as one of the most valuable tools for understanding the human personality.

Today, the Enneagram is a powerful system that describes nine distinct and fundamentally different patterns of thinking, behaving, and feeling. Each of the nine patterns is built upon a definite and distinctive perceptual framework, a filter through which the world is viewed and through which sensory data is processed. This filter determines how one sees everything and what one pays attention to. At the heart of each of the nine patterns is a fundamental thinking/feeling posture, or belief, concerning what one needs in life in order to survive and be fulfilled. Simply stated, every one of us developed one of these nine patterns for the primary purpose of protecting a specific portion of ourselves that felt particularly vulnerable as our personalities were developing. Individuals who discover their Enneagram personality types, as we did, quickly discover invaluable information about their whole selves—what motivates them, how they relate to themselves and to others, and how they deal with the vast array of circumstances they face in life.

Books on the Enneagram can be found today in most public libraries and bookstores in the United States and Canada. The works of Dr. Helen Palmer (Berkeley, CA.), Don Richard Riso (Boston, MA.), and Dr. Virginia Price and Dr. David Daniels (Stanford University) have provided to us the most current and comprehensive information about the Enneagram, its history and its value. To obtain further information, please contact:

Meisburg Communications
P.O. Box 10162
Tallahassee, Florida 32302

Bibliography

Bennett, J. G. *Sex* (York Beach, Maine: Samuel Weisner, 1981).

Blanck, Rubin and Gertrude Blanck. *Beyond Ego Psychology: Developmental Object Relations Theory* (New York: Columbia University Press, 1986).

Bly, Robert. *A Little Book on the Human Shadow*. William Booth, Ed. (San Francisco: Harper & Row, 1988).

Bourgeault, Cynthia. *Love Is Stronger Than Death* (New York: Bell Tower, 1999).

Bowen, Murray. *Family Therapy in Clinical Practice* (New York: J. Aronson, 1978).

Bowby, John. *Attachment and Loss* (New York: Basic Books, 1969).

Bowby, John. *A Secure Base: Parent-Child Attachment and Healthy Human Development* (New York: Basic Books, 1988).

Buber, Martin. *I and Thou* (New York: Charles Scribner and Son, 1958).

Campbell, Joseph. *The Power of Myth* (New York; Doubleday, 1988).

Craig, W. J. ed. *William Shakespeare: The Histories and Poems* (London: Oxford University Press, 1912).

Dickinson, Emily. *Selected Poems and Letters of Emily Dickinson* (New York; Doubleday, 1959).

Donne, John. *The Complete Poetry and Selected Prose*. Chas. M. Coffin, ed. (New York: Modern Library, 1952).

Foundation for Inner Peace, A Course in Miracles (Glen Ellen, Calif.: The Foundation, 1992).

Fowler, Connie May. *Before Women Had Wings* (New York: G. M. Putnam's Sons, 1996).

Gottman, J. et al., *A Couple's Guide to Communication* (Champaign, IL: Research Press, 1976).

Gottman, J. *Why Marriages Succeed or Fail* (New York: Simon & Schuster, 1994).

Gottman, J. and Nan Silver. *The Seven Principles for Making Marriage Work* (New York: Crown Publishers Incorporated, 1999).

Gottman, J. and Nan Silver. *Why Marriages Succeed or Fail and How You Can Make Yours Last* (New York: Simon & Schuster, 1995).

Hall, James A. *The Jungian Experience: Analysis and Individuation* (Toronto, Canada: Inner City Books, 1986).

Hendricks, Gay and Kathlyn Hendricks. *Conscious Loving: The Journey to Co-commitment* (New York: Bantam Books, 1990).

Hendrix, Harville. *Getting the Love You Want—A Guide for Couples* (New York: Henry Holt & Co., 1988).

Hendrix, Harville. *Giving the Love That Heals: A Guide for Parents* (New York: Pocket Books, 1997).

Hendrix, Harville. *Keeping the Love You Find: A Guide for Singles* (New York: Pocket Books, 1993).

Hind, R. A. *Biological Basis for Human Social Behavior* (New York: McGraw-Hill, 1974).

Huffines, L. *Connecting With All the People in Your Life* (San Francisco: Harper & Row, 1986).

James, Henry. "The Beast in the Jungle." In *Fifteen Short Stories* (New York: Bantam Books, 1961).

Johnson, Robert A. *Ecstasy: Understanding the Psychology of Joy* (San Francisco: Harper & Row, 1987).

Johnson, Robert A. *Transformation: Understanding the Three Levels of Masculine Consciousness* (San Francisco: Harper San Francisco, 1993).

Johnson, Robert A. *We, Understanding the Psychology of Romantic Love* (San Francisco: Harper & Row, 1998).

Johnson, Robert A. and Jerry M. Ruhl. *Balancing Heaven and Earth: A Memoir* (San Francisco: Harper San Francisco, 1998).

Jung, C. G. *Analytical Psychology: Its Theory and Practice: The Tavistock Lectures* (New York: Pantheon Books, 1968).

Jung, C. G. *The Archetypes and the Collective Unconscious*. Trans. R. F. C. Hull (Princeton, N. J.: Princeton University Press, 1959).

Jung, C. G. *Dreams*. Trans. by R. F. C. Hull (Princeton, N.J.: Princeton University Press, 1974).

Jung, C. G. *Man and His Symbols* (Garden City, N. Y., Doubleday, 1964).

Jung, C. G. *Memories, Dreams, Reflections*. Aniela Jaffe, ed. (London: Collins Fontana Library, 1967).

Jung, C. G. *Portable Jung*, Joseph Campbell, ed. (New York: Viking Press, 1971).

Keen, Sam. *To Love and Be Loved* (New York: Bantam Books, 1997).

Kerr, Michael E. *Family Evaluation: An Approach Based on Bowen* (New York: Norton, 1988).

Kurtz, Ernest, and Kathlyn Ketchum. *The Spirituality of Imperfection* (New York: Bantam Books, 1992).

Levine, Stephen, and Ondrea Levine. *Embracing the Beloved: Relationship as a Path of Awakening* (New York: Doubleday, 1995).

Lewis, C. S. *Mere Christianity: A Revised and Enlarged Edition, with a New Introduction of the Three Books, The Case for Christianity, Christian Behavior, and Beyond Personality* (New York: Macmillan, 1952).

Lewis, C. S. *The Screwtape Letters* (New York: Touchstone Books, Simon & Schuster, 1996).

Mahler, Margaret S. *The Psychological Birth of the Human Infant: Symbiosis and Individuation* (New York: Basic Books, 1975).

Main, H. Stadtman. "Innocent Response to Rejection and Physical Contact by the Mother: Aggression, Avoidance and Contact." In *Journal of Academic Child Psychiatry* 20 (1981), 292-307.

Miller, Alice. *The Drama of the Gifted Child: The Search for the True Self*. Trans. Ruth Ward (New York: Basic Books, 1994).

Mindell, Arnold. *Dreambody, The Body's Role in Revealing the Self*. Sisa Sternback-Scott and Becky Goodman, eds. (Santa Monica, California: Sigo Press, 1982).

Moore, Thomas. *Care of the Soul: A Guide for Cultivating Depth and Sacredness in Everyday Life* (New York: Harper Collins, c1992).

Moore, Thomas. *Soul Mates: Honoring the Mysteries of Love and Relationship* (New York: Harper Collins Publishers, 1994).

Norris, Kathleen. *The Cloister Walk* (New York: Riverhead Books, 1996).

Nouwen, Henri. *The Return of "The Prodigal Son"* (New York: Image Books, 1992).

Papero, Daniel V. *Bowen Family Systems* (Boston, Mass.: Allyn and Bacon, 1990).

Pearson, Carol. *Awakening the Heroes* (San Francisco: Harper, 1991).

Peck, Scott. *The Road Less Traveled* (New York: Simon & Schuster, 1978).

Polk, William R. *Polk's Folly: An American Family History* (New York: Doubleday, 2000).

Rilke, Rainer Maria. *Letters to a Young Poet*. Trans. Steven Mitchell (New York: Vantage Books, 1986).

Ryle, Anthony. *Frames and Cages: The Repertory Grid Approach to Human Understanding* (London: Sussex University Press, 1975).

Ryle, Anthony. *Neurosis in the Ordinary Family: A Psychiatric Survey* (London: Tavistock Publications, 1967).

Schnarch, David Morris. *Passionate Marriage: Love, Sex, and Intimacy in Emotionally Committed Relationships* (New York: W. W. Norton, 1997).

Sharp, Daryl. *Jung Lexicon: A Primer of Terms and Concepts* (Toronto, Canada: Inner City Books, 1991).

Spitz, Rene A. and W. Godfrey Cobliner. *The First Year of Life: A Psychoanalytic Study of Normal and Deviant Development of Object Relations* (New York: International Universities Press, 1965).

Sullivan, Harry Stack. *Personal Psychopathology: Early Formulations* (New York: Norton, 1953).

Sullivan, Harry Stack. *The Interpersonal Theory of Psychiatry*. Helen Swick Perry and Mary Ladd Gawel, eds. (New York: Norton, 1953).

Thomas, Nancy. *When Love Is Not Enough* (PO Box 2812, Glenwood Springs, CO 81602).

Vanderwall, Francis. *Freedom From Fear: A Way Through the Ways of Jesus the Christ* (Lafayette, Louisiana: Acadian House, 1999).

Vaughan, Frances E. and Roger N. Walsh, eds. *Accept This Gift: Selections from a Course in Miracles* (Los Angeles: J. P. Tarcher, 1992).

Woodman, Marion. *The Pregnant Virgin: A Process of Psychological Transformation* (Toronto, Canada: Inner City Books, 1985).

Yeats, William Butler. *Selected Poems and Two Plays*. M .L. Rosenthal, ed. (New York, Macmillan, 1962).

Index

THE NEW MARRIAGE

Transcending the
Happily-Ever-After Myth

How to Put Your Relationship
Back on Track

Marriage and family therapists Linda
and Robert Miles offer the answers
to your questions, and provide the
tools that will empower couples to
transform their relationships, move
beyond Hollywood-inspired, happily-
ever-after fantasies, and learn to create
realistic, long-term adult relationships.

You can thrive as a couple if you're willing to do what it takes.

- Make your marriage succeed, even though seven out of ten couples who marry today will eventually divorce.

- Learn how to identify and overcome the emotional problems that arise from marital troubles, and use that knowledge to achieve a long-lasting union.

- Strengthen yourself and your partner instead of helplessly watching your marriage dissolve.

"The New Marriage provides a wonderful, innovative model for helping develop and maintain healthy relationships. Drs. Linda and Robert Miles offer a visionary approach for today's couples. We highly recommend this book and commend the authors . . ."

James H. Akin, ACSW, Executive Director,
& Lynn M. Wray, LCSW, Coordinator of Continuing Education,
National Association of Social Workers, Florida Chapter

Professional therapists, Linda and Robert Miles have each worked in the mental health field for over thirty years. Married for more than ten years, they are deeply committed to helping other couples achieve rewarding relationships. Linda Miles has written many articles about communications skills and relationships, and co-authored *Amanda Salamander Discovers the Secret of Happily-Ever-After*, a realistic fable created to help children develop healthier expectations of relationships. Robert Miles is Senior Psychiatrist for the Mental Health Program Office, Department of Children and Families, for the State of Florida. In addition to private practice, he has consulted for numerous agencies, done administrative and clinical hospital work, and been co-therapist with his wife in work with couples. The Mileses live in Tallahassee, Florida, and have three sons and three young grandchildren.

ISBN 1-879384-39-6

61995

9 781879 384392